◆—✕—◆

Dear Stress,
I'M BREAKING UP
WITH YOU.

◆—✕—◆

Dear Stress, I'M BREAKING UP WITH YOU.

The Woman's Guide To End Internal And External Pressures While On Her Way To Success.

By Ky-Lee Hanson

Contributing Authors:
Stephanie Butler, Eva Macias, Amanda Yeatman,
Tania J Moraes-Vaz, Kathryn Yeatman, Karina K Ullrich,
Dr. Supriya Gade, Kyla Thomson, Sunit Suchdev, Rusiana T Mannarino,
Kimberly Francis, AJ Roy, Patricia Yeatman, Kelly Rolfe,
Michelle Zubrinich & Dr. Lauren E. Karatanevski.

Golden Brick Road
Publishing House

(C) 2017 by Ky-Lee Hanson

Published by GOLDEN BRICK ROAD PUBLISHING HOUSE

For any information regarding permission contact
Ky-Lee Hanson via
kylee@gbrpublicationsagency.com

ISBN: 978-1-988736-00-6

First publication, 2017

Book cover design by
www.designisreborn.com

www.dearstressbook.com

Contents

Preface

DEAR STRESS, I'M Breaking Up With You is a compilation book written by women for women. My name is Ky-Lee Hanson and I am the lead author, visionary and compiler of the "Dear" Women Guide Book Series.

I am the, "1. Say Yes 2. Tell the World 3. Figure it Out." - Eric Worre, kind of person. I've always had a goal to change society for the better. A big task, I know. They say only crazy people have the ability to change the world, and my dreams have always been "out there".

Throughout my life, I have worn many hats and also many masks. I have appeared as many different people, most times, often not recognizing myself. I would say at those moments; life was the hardest. Whenever my vision has been blurred - I felt like I was bushwhacking, instead of walking my Golden Brick Road. Now, looking back at those times, I can say that I was depressed. I was anxious and stressed out. I was lost.

This book came to me on a night like that. I had recently jumped in with our publisher to lead and create a co-author book. I had been published before as a co-author and now, I was taking the leadership and doing it myself. I didn't know what I was doing, but I knew the overall purpose was to create opportunity for other women. It would be similar to what I had experienced from being a published coauthor, but now with my own touch. It opens doors. I saw the big picture of inspiring the co-authors, helping them develop and as a result, we help our readers. I have always been about inspiring an individual and their ability to then inspire a community. It is the inspiration trickle effect. The week between the day I jumped in with the publisher by paying a hefty deposit, to the day I named this book, was an extremely hard week. I found out that not only was my knee painful, internally bruising and swelling, but my meniscus was torn, again. I left my [distraction] job to pursue the unknown and put 200% back into my various businesses which made my spouse and I unsure about what was going to happen to us financially. He booked me a flight to visit him where he works in NYC, my favorite place on Earth! Last minute, I had to cancel because my knee was in excruciating pain and the process of traveling with a limp, a brace, ice pack and painkillers was not my idea of fun. I created anxiety and stress in my mind by playing out the, "I can't", "what if", "could cause more pain", scenarios in my mind.

That night as I laid on my couch crying in physical and emotional pain, feeling so sorry for myself, I decided this was what the book needed to be about. Breaking up with stress! To stop being a victim of my own mind and to stop letting jobs, finance, physical pain and other external crap control me. The next day, since I was staying in town, I went out to support an event hosted by an entrepreneurial friend of mine. I was proud of her for doing so and she is in this book, Michelle Zubrinich. It was a beautiful event, all except for the guest speaker. As a Gemini, I have two very strong sides. One is an optimistic ball of awesomeness and the other is a miserable sack of anxiety. Well luckily, optimistic was out that day! The speaker's teachings did very little for me. The message the guest speaker was trying to project was not well received. I had honestly heard the material before, time and time again. However, I did receive a very big lesson that day. I CAN do what this speaker does and I believe I can do it better. I am meant to be up there speaking. It was time for me to step up and lead. To really lead women in business. I was meant to be creating material and inspiring others to do the same. To be the best version of themselves. To share what is unique in them and help all women admire their own uniqueness. That day, I went from a hobby coach in network marketing to a fully rounded Motivational Mentor and Business Creationist.

I got to work and in three weeks, I had the book concept and mission in place. I had my list of dream coauthors. Most of them met with me! A few of them joined. I had many more chapters to fill… over the next two weeks I would speak with almost 100 inspiring women. It was stimulating, yet exhausting. Everything came together. I found my aces and was committed to making this the best experience for everyone, and because of all those who said no to this opportunity, the fire to go Wall Street Journal Best Seller, was even stronger. I will bring my vision to life and show people my strength, and I will do it by bringing others up with me! People do not always hear our message, but they always see our actions.

I encourage everyone to read this book in whichever order and under whichever conditions they most enjoy. We designed it with the busy person in mind, as well as, the ADHD all-over-the-place reader, and the leisurely reader. We have highlighted key points and provided takeaway tips. This book is designed to impact your life and help you make change. The book can be read from start to finish and you will hear from me between sections to check in with you. This book can also be read by section or individual chapter. You can jump around and take what you need, as you need it, on the subject specific to your current development. Each chapter is written by an expert in that subject and each chapter is an inclusive story all on its own. ExpertEnough.com and Udemy conducted a study and the results said it takes 29 days or 700 hours to become an expert in Yoga or 26,800 hours to become an expert in Economics.[1] TheMuse.com says 95% of people have the capacity to learn and acquire knowledge in ANY field of study. Overall, the consensus is the 10,000 Hour Rule Theory; expertise takes 10,000 hours of focus and practice on the topic.[2] Our authors have LIVED. They have lived through stress, pain, happiness, transformation and have helped others. We are experts at life and certain areas within life and society. I believe you are also an expert at something and I encourage you to reach out to every single author in this book that resonates with you and reach out to me if you have a story you need help to cultivate and share. Get a grasp on reality with

Patricia Yeatman, Kelly Rolfe, Tania Jane Moraes-Vaz and Karina K Ullrich in our first section, *The Weight Within*. We then move onto the next section by putting priorities and *Family Matter*s in check with Kathryn Yeatman, Stephanie Butler, Sunit Suchdev, and Eva Macias. Health is such a big factor in happiness. We address this in the *Healing The Body with Knowledge,* section with Dr. Lauren E. Karatanevski, Kimberly Francis RN., Amanda Yeatman CHC., Medical Momma Kyla Thomson, and from a Survivor and Thriver perspective with AJ Roy. There comes a point in life where we must stand up and say, *"I am MORE than just a Girl"*. This statement titles our section where we dive into stereotypes and male dominance with Dr. Supriya Gade, Michelle Zubrinich and Rusiana T Mannarino. Once we are amped up from all this knowledge, we can apply our new outlook on life onto our external world. You will find me at the end to send you off with a motivational kick and help you pave new positive expectations of your life and to fall in love with each day you have on this journey to success!

Ky-Lee Hanson
kylee@gbrpublicationsagency.com

---

[1] How Many Hours Does It Take To Become An Expert? (n.d) *How Many Hours Does It Take To Become An Expert?* Retrieved from expertenough.com Online http://expertenough.com/2442/10000-hours-to-become-an-expert-infographic

[2] Jessen, Catherine. *How To Become An Expert At Anything*. Retrieved from www.themuse.com Online https://www.themuse.com/advice/how-to-become-an-expert-at-anything

Introduction

WHY WAS I destined to write a book on Breaking up with Stress? Is it because I have it all figured out? That is only partially true. I still experience bad stress. Sometimes, I want to scream, sometimes I want to break a dish and sometimes, I am exhausted from my stress leading to depression which looks like moping about, my hair not done, a bag of chips and lots of couch time and sleep. Goodbye World, see you in a week! While interviewing coauthors for this book, conducting research and sharing the book concept with friends, family and clients, I came to find that most people often feel similar emotions, act in similar negative ways and refer to it as a "rollercoaster". Let's turn to The Canadian Mental Health Association for a minute. Their website states, "We all talk about stress, but we're not always clear about what it is. Stress comes from both the good and the bad things that happen to us. If we didn't feel any stress, we wouldn't be alive! Stress may feel overwhelming at times, but there are many strategies to help you take control… Stress can be difficult to understand. The emotional chaos it causes can make our daily lives miserable. It can also decrease our physical health, sometimes drastically. Strangely, we are not always aware that we are under stress. The habits, attitudes, and signs that can alert us to problems may be hard to recognize because they have become so familiar." Stress looks different on each of us, which is why this book is more powerful through the voice of many, our coauthors.

There is likely a connection between stress and illness. Theories of the stress–illness link suggest that both acute and chronic stress can cause illness, and several studies found such a link. [1] According to these theories, both kinds of stress can lead to changes in behavior and in physiology. Behavioral changes can be smoking, eating habits and physical activity. Physiological changes can be changes in sympathetic activation or hypothalamic pituitary adrenocorticoid activation, and immunological function. [1] However, there is much variability in the link between stress and illness. [2] Chronic stress and a lack of coping resources available or used by an individual can often lead to the development of psychological issues such as depression and anxiety. [3] This is particularly true regarding chronic stressors. These are stressors that may not be as intense as an acute stressor like a natural disaster or a major accident, but they persist over longer periods of time.

I am not a person that embraces illness. I am not ok with being off work or taking one's opinion on MY health. I want to take care of myself. I want to be healthy. I want to feel good. I want to control my life. I believe I can do that and have proved it to myself time and time again. That simple. There is no control when tied down in pain, illness or stress. Am I against medicine? No, of course not. However, it is easy to let disease consume us and sometimes doctors don't have all the answers. We are still learning as a society and science is developing daily. My studies and interests within Biochemistry, Sociology and Psychology have led me to ponder many social norms. Most people reading this book lived through decades where stress was almost seen as "cool". It was cool to be grunge, emo, angry, stressed and broke. It was cool to be tough, strong and show no emotion. "Happy people are fake." Any of this sound familiar to 80's and 90's kids? Science now shows links between the mind and the immune system, as well as how our environment affects our epigenome. Could our attitude be making our body sick? Science seems to think so. Is that always the case? No. Sometimes, life doesn't make sense and it is not fair. In each situation though, if we work together and do not accept things at face value but for what lies deeper, what is the cause to the effect, together we can grow at rapid speed. We are in fact, living in the Knowledge Age. ShiftThinking.org states, "Knowledge is no longer being thought of as 'stuff' that is developed (and stored) in the minds of experts, represented in books, and classified into disciplines. Instead, it is now thought of as being like a form of energy, as a system of networks and flows – something that does things, or makes things happen. The Knowledge Age is defined—and valued—not for what it is, but for what it can do. It is produced, not by individual experts, but by 'collectivizing intelligence' – that is, groups of people with complementary expertise who collaborate for specific purposes. These changes have major implications for our education system."

In our external world of relationships with others, sometimes relationships need to evolve or change, and sometimes you need to breakup with that relationship. It is the same with stress and our inner emotions. Stress has been made into a public health enemy, but new research suggests that stress may only be bad for you if you believe that to be true. Psychologist Kelly McGonigal urges us to see stress as a positive, and introduces us to an unsung mechanism for stress reduction: reaching out to others. A study was done over 8 years in the United States, to see how harmful stress is to human health. The people who believed that stress was harmful to health opposed to those that did not see it as harmful to health, had a 43% increased risk in dying. People that did not view it as harmful to health although they experienced high levels of stress, had no increase in risk of death. Kelley McGonigal asks, "Can changing how you think about stress, make you healthier? Here the science says, "Yes". [4] This book is a guide to ending pressures and breaking up with overwhelming-stress. We offer you real stories and a community of authors that are reaching out to you and inviting you to reach back.

I've often been told that I am stressed. I have been told I am too busy, that I am doing too much and that I need to take time for myself. Sometimes, I am flabbergasted at this. Some people don't understand that I enjoy "stress"; the good kind that is. The stress I face is making myself a priority within a society that does not value that. They see it as being selfish, hardworking, closed off, busy, naive, optimistic and "not realistic". We have been taught that our boss, spouse, job, friends, children, savings and household should all come before us as an individual; if these things are not first, we are not responsible. Being happy and optimistic is often looked at as having less intelligence and having a detachment for reality. Our emotions affect our outlook on the world. We can't always control how we feel, but when we can choose to see light even in a dark situation, as stressful as it may be, is there not benefit to this? Are we kidding ourselves? I enjoy being nervous, I translate it to excitement and a sign that I am on the right path. The feeling of scarcity means I need to find more, not hold back what I already have. I've been challenged to find more and since I have found it in the past, I know my ability to be resourceful. I am hungry for more and I enjoy creating. Naturally, that makes me a project-oriented person. Projects come with deadlines and deadlines translate to pressure for most people. To me, deadlines mean it is finally done and now I have the desired outcome. The way I look at stress is different than most people. How do we do this? How do we look at stress in a good way? Maybe we have made stress an enemy and there is a lot of bad energy around that word. We need to break up with, and end that stigma. We have to take the control back. The law of the universe is that every negative has a positive, it's science. Can we benefit from stressful situations? Can we benefit from heartache, growing pains, disease and self-agony? Can we find the good and come out stronger? Most importantly, how can we keep control? I have found a simple answer to it all: self-development. Create a habit of reading, listening and asking questions. Strive to give yourself everything you desire and first focus on becoming that version of yourself who has it. Since I am a work-first and project-oriented type of person, I have turned my needs into my wants. I turned my need to get healthy into something I wanted. Not only did I want to feel good, everyone wants that. But I wanted to help others, I wanted to lead, I wanted to make money and I wanted positive friends. I made health my business. Something else that I wanted was more time to read, write, improve my grammar skills and learn to speak publicly. I began to join and soon lead co-author books, just like this one. Again, I made my interest my business. There is no guilt in putting time and money into a hobby if you believe it will help you grow and also help you earn. It is a win for you and your family when you can offer new found knowledge and happiness. All of this elevates bad stress and helps you to be excited for the future.

What does your stress-free version of yourself look like? What does she wear, what does she eat, who are her friends, what does her office look like? If you imagine yourself as a person that doesn't let bad experiences control her, in theory, that person is happy. Are you strong and ready to seize the day? Will you live your life or are you living in someone else's world? Where is the control? Can you find the good in each situation, even within the bad? How can it make you stronger and more resourceful? Or maybe you are exhausted. Let us help you recharge and develop a new outlook on stress and life, and give you a motivational kick to become the best version of yourself.

[1] Herbert, T. B.; Cohen, S. (1993). "Stress and immunity in humans: a meta-analytic review". Psychosomatic Medicine. 55 (4): 364–379. doi:10.1097/00006842-199307000-00004

[2] Jump up ^ Ogden, J. (2007). Health Psychology: a textbook (4th ed.), pages 281–282 New York: McGraw-Hill ISBN 0335214711

[3] Schlotz W, Yim IS, Zoccola PM, Jansen L, Schulz P (2011). The perceived stress reactivity scale: Measurement invariance, stability, and validity in three countries. Psychol Assess. (pp. 80–94)

[4] McGonigal, Kelly. How To Make Stress Your Friend. Retrieved from ted.com Online https://www.ted.com/talks/kelly_mcgonigal_how_to_make_stress_your friend?language=en#t-120180

Section 1

The Weight Within

featuring
Patricia Yeatman, Kelly Rolfe, Tania Jane Moraes-Vaz
and Karina K Ullrich

Editorial commentary by Ky-Lee Hanson

CAN WE CHANGE our state of mind to have a different outlook on life and create a different outcome? Of course. We are capable of creating inner peace or inner war. External factors play a role, but if we start within the self and spend the time to learn about and understand ourselves, we may find our reality looking a bit different.

Anxiety, depression, lack of self-confidence and little self-awareness could be clouding our judgement. The judgement of ourselves, of life and other people. Maybe what we perceive is not quite true. When we take the time to understand our truth with a balanced mind and look at our life from various angles, we can then own our truth, and get rid of what is false.

Maybe you think you are ugly, but are you? Really? Of course not. Stop owning that and own what is factual about you. "Beautiful" is a feeling, "Ugly" is a feeling. What are you on the inside? How do you feel? When we accept it as a feeling instead of a truth, from there we can work to change from the inside out. If there are areas that are not quite clear, for example, you have an interest in something but have no experience or understanding of it, accept that you need to gain knowledge in that subject, begin to learn and then that interest becomes a part of your truth. We are creatures of habit and it is easy to get into a routine, sometimes an unfavorable one, but it is also easy to make happiness a habit once we shift our focus there. Our routine IS our life, so we should make sure our activities and tasks are worth our time.

You ARE capable, yet many things may be standing in your way. Make sure that YOU are not one of those things. Be your biggest cheerleader instead of your biggest critic. Now, how exactly do we get that mean part of us to go away? The one who tells us we can't, the one who tells us we are ugly or not good enough. The one who tells us we don't have the time or worth. The truth is, time is ticking and we DO have unique worth. Not one other person is just the same.

Can we just break up with this inner mean girl already? Yes! But how? In this section, come and learn how to break up with your inner critic and mean girl. Patricia guides us on how to seize the day as the clock keeps ticking away, while Kelly help us identify that our inner critic can be silenced when we learn how to consciously evolve our thought process from a negative one to a positive one, and Tania teaches us when and how to say NO. And lastly, Karina shows us how to embrace and surround ourselves with positive and strategic influences in our life that will help us grow constructively on a consistently positive basis.

Chapter 1

Tic Toc Tic Toc Tic Toc

by Patricia Yeatman

*"What do YOU hear? The sound of time passing by – passing YOU by,
an external clock, an internal clock or a time bomb. "*
~ Patricia Yeatman

Patricia Yeatman

Patricia Yeatman is a mother of four (Erin 44, Kathryn 42, Christopher 37 and Amanda 35), a wife to Mark, a grandmother (Nana) of 9 (Makayla, Jack, Avrey, Hunter, Sophia, Charlie, Emma, Tom and Sadie), a friend to many, a professional actor since 1986 and a Network Marketing Professional. She is 65 years old and proud of it. She believes that life is a gigantic gift that too many take for granted, herself included, until these last few years. She is fiercely loyal to her family and they have always been, and will always be, her priority, but she has now learned that taking care of herself is crucial to her well-being.

ig: @patriciayeatman | t: @patriciayeatman | fb: @patriciayeatman9

STRESS IS DEFINED as, "A state of mental tension and worry caused by problems in your life, work, etc. something that causes strong feelings of worry or anxiety, physical force or pressure". Anything here sound familiar? The American Institute of Stress gives this definition, "Stress is not a useful term for scientists because it is such a highly subjective phenomenon that it defies definition."

Well, to that I say, whatever *your* definition, we have all encountered it. Some live with it, some give into it, and some work to get rid of it. The latter is where I sit or at least where I try to. That is not to say I don't experience high levels of "it", but I have learned to be more aware of its' knocking at my life door. My solution/resolution, is to live in the moment, not in the moments that *follow*, but the one you're IN. This is a work in progress. I am a work in progress.

It begins with the realization that we all have it; you may hear some say, "I'm so busy I can't think straight", "I feel like I'm running in circles", "I hardly have time to breathe". There are many forms, many ways to express it, describe it, but we all experience this at one time or another, in our personal and professional lives.

At this very moment of writing this, I am in the throes of "decluttering/downsizing" as my husband and I decided to leave our beautiful home of 28 years to begin a new chapter. This has been/is very emotional for me as 28 years in one home brings with it many memories, but it also contains many material "things" that I have accumulated over the years; things I need to get rid of, to clear my physical space, and also my mental space. I realize that it's also time to "declutter" my thoughts, patterns, beliefs and fears, and realize that the stress of maintaining this large home could be alleviated by moving into a smaller home that would not have as many demands. You could say I'm a little stressed. (Insert laughter). So what do I do? I agree to co-author a book. (Insert an emoji face with big disbelieving eyes) I am still surprised, shocked and pretty darn proud of myself for once again saying "yes" to something brand new. It scares me, and I think that's a good thing. So…. stressful? (Insert laughter again) Sure, but I am using that to fuel me, not cripple me.

When all is said and done, I want to look back at my life and see that I truly "lived."

I am a 65-year-old woman, a proud wife, mother of 4 and grandmother of 9, a friend, an actor and an entrepreneur. I love my family more than any other thing on this earth and I know that by dealing with my "stresses" in a positive way, I am giving them a better wife, a better mother and a better Nana. I want to give them that gift. I have not always succeeded. I have definitely encountered a lot of the stresses that many of my beautiful co-author colleagues, friends and family have, or are, encountering. Motherhood, Marriage, Divorce, Moving, Death, Health Issues, etc. and the truth is that some of the stress from *dealing* with some of these issues, causes *other* stresses. When that happens, it is not pretty!

Recognizing and acknowledging that the sense of "strangulation" that we can get from these factors can cripple us or fuel us, is the first step towards controlling and hopefully, stopping this runaway train in its tracks before it does too much damage. It manifests itself in so many ways, emotionally and physically.

Meditation, affirmations, therapy are a few of the ways we can stop this "thing" in its tracks, otherwise it is easy to fall into the "my life is shit" hole. Put your big girl panties on and kick that "thing" to the curb or it will start to rule your life and then you will live in fear, worried about trying anything new, worried about making a mistake, worried about "living" the life you were given to live.

"In the end, it's not the years in your life that count. It's the life in your years,"
Abraham Lincoln

Even the greatest events in our lives cause us "stress" but the truth is, good or bad, it is all stress. Getting married, having children, having your child get married, achieving a degree in University, to name a few are all wonderful events and moments but stressful? Hell yeah! Stress is stress. Good or Bad. Taking a moment to recognize that stress need not be a renter in your mind, and not allowing yourself to be a landlord and allowing it to reside within you, will allow you to evict the squatter and move past the darkness and into the light. This will take work, but it will be worth it.

As a professional actor, a profession I absolutely love and will never give up, I "live in the moment" when I am on the stage, as one must to truly give our audiences a truthful performance. My goal is to live my life the same way, truthful and in the moment. Enter my Network Marketing business for which I will always be extremely grateful. Again, something brand new, new territory, bringing up new fears that I had squelched. It is a little scary at first, then you realize what a gift it is to be in complete control of your future and to be able to offer that gift to others. When I made that decision 6 years ago, to venture into the absolute unknown – the world of Network Marketing – I had absolutely no idea how it would change me and help me evolve into a better person. It has enriched my life in so many ways.

There is such freedom in that, and yet, stress keeps creeping in every now and again, from the pressures I put on *myself.* When I recognize that is happening, I switch gears and remind myself of how *grateful* I am for what I am doing, how proud I am of myself for taking that leap into the complete unknown, a business I knew absolutely nothing about, for trusting that this was a way for me to have freedom and choice in my life. You may have heard this saying before, "Develop an attitude of gratitude". Even on those days where you are crankier than a rhino in heat, take a breath and remind yourself of what you have. Look at the smallest things and be grateful for them. Take a moment right now to think of three things that you are grateful for today, at this moment. Feel the difference in your breathing. Force yourself to smile and your brain will translate that action into an emotion of happiness. Start to laugh. No, I mean it. Force yourself to laugh right now. Keep going and watch how, within seconds, you are laughing whole heartedly, almost uncontrollably and if anyone else is around you, *they* will start laughing because YOU are laughing. It's contagious, like yawning! Stress has no chance to take hold when you take control of your thoughts and physical actions.

It pains me that so many my age, and *younger*, spend so much time "stressing" about getting older, they are missing out on precious moments of "*living*", moments that are beautiful *because* we are older. Hey, don't get me wrong, this ageing thing comes with a lot of "crap"; the person in the mirror seems to have gotten more wrinkles overnight, a little arthritis might be setting in, there will be days when your back hurts, your feet hurt, hell you feel like you might be falling apart, and your doctor tells you that at "your age" you need a shingles shot, a flu shot, a pneumonia shot. Whaaattt?? Helloooo Mrs. Pin cushion. So where is the upside of this you ask? Well, here in Canada, you also get an "Old Age Pension". A little monthly present for living this long. Helloooo! Thank you. I remind myself that I am one of the lucky ones. Again, gratitude. Many never got to receive that cheque, never got to see their grandchildren grow up, heck some won't get to see their *children* grow up. I have been reminded way too many times about how short life is and what a gift it is.

We have no control over when that will happen, but we can certainly control how we choose to live our lives up to that point.

Some spend their lives *waiting to retire* because they have worked their entire lives – some at jobs they loved, some at jobs they hated, but all for that almighty *security* of the pay cheque (you know, that sum of money that you get when you show up, when *they* tell you to, vacation when *they* tell you that you can, feel guilty if you have to leave a sick child but you *can't call in sick* because *they* won't like it.) Hey, if you love your job, that is fantastic! However, there are many who don't; who spend their time "wishing" they were doing something else. Time is passing, and trust me when I tell you that it seems to pass a hundred times faster as you age, so find something that makes you happy, that gives you fulfillment. Don't be an "ironing board" (a surfboard that gave up their dreams). Listen, you may be looking forward to "retirement" but are "stressed" about it, because you are now going to be living on 40% of your wage. There is life waiting for those who are worried. There are ways to alleviate that stress. Personally, "retirement" is not a word I will ever use for myself. I think of "retiring" as "going to bed" "going to sleep" and for me that translates to "lying down and not being active". I have no way of knowing if I will be forced into that one day, but until that day comes, I want to be "alive", "awake", "aware".

What I want to say is this, "Don't let your age stop you from *starting* your life!!!" It's time to stop stressing about the seconds, minutes, hours, months, years that are going by, worrying about "the time you have *left*", the time it takes to learn something new, the time it takes to plan another adventure, and treasure the *gift* that you have been given, and the moments you are living right now.

Take some risks in your life for heaven's sake!

Stop living where you think it is less "stressful", where it is "safer", in that zone of "If I don't fly, I won't get killed in a plane crash", "if I don't tell a joke, I won't risk them not laughing", "if I don't tell someone I love them, I won't risk rejection" and so on. There will always be elements of *bad* stress in our lives to keep us on our toes, I suspect, but I believe we need to acknowledge it, identify it, and move out of it. I challenge you to grab life by the proverbial "balls" and get out of your own way. Do something out of your current "comfort zone". Step out of that area that keeps you "safe" and venture into something new. It will breathe new life into you. Be brave, adventurous, open to learning and loving.

Wise words from a Sagittarian philosopher: Many people seem to live their lives as if this were a dress rehearsal. This is not a dress rehearsal. This is the real thing. The curtain is up and all the stops are out. You are alive. Start living. And I will add be "grateful", be "kind to your body", be "kind" to yourself and others", be "aware". Embrace your life and all that comes with it and take charge. The best is yet to come. Tic Toc people! Tic Toc!

"Don't watch the clock; do what it does.
Keep going." – Sam Levenson

Chapter 2

Breaking Up With Your Inner Mean Girl!

by Kelly Rolfe

"I refuse to be the girl who didn't pursue her passions because she didn't have enough belief in herself."
~ CreativeBrandista.com

Kelly Rolfe

Kelly has always known she wanted to help people. This lead her to a career in children's mental health. She has been trained in multiple therapies to help children, youth and their families to lead a life of mental wellness. She has strived to help families reach their client-centered goals with passion, enthusiasm and care.

In more recent years, Kelly endured some challenges in her personal life. She became a single mother to her beautiful daughter, Ryenne. Throughout these difficult times, Kelly was compelled to start a journey of health and fitness. As Kelly transformed her physical self, she began to understand that overall wellness has a much deeper component, and she began to work on her internal self. As she dug deep into her negative thought patterns (or "mean girl"), she began to heal and transform while learning love and acceptance of who she was. Through her personal journey, she found a true passion for helping other women on their journey of health, wellness and self-love. This passion led her to become a health and fitness coach. Through this opportunity, Kelly has helped countless women transform their lives. She has not only supported their fitness journey, but become a leader in finding self-love. Throughout her personal and professional journey, Kelly has set out to live her dream of helping people achieve self-love and overall wellness. To truly love one's self, you must first accept who you are while working towards what you want to be.

ig: @mama_gets_fit_and_fab | fb: facebook.com/kellygetsfit2016

GROWING UP, WE were given a very specific lists of "shoulds". We should act like a girl, then a lady, get good grades, go to college, get a good job, get married, have a family, etc. I don't know about you but that list of "shoulds" didn't exactly lead me to a journey of happiness and success. It led me to believe that if I didn't fit into that mold, then I wasn't good enough. This feeling of not being good enough begins to develop within us at a very young age and if you're anything like me, carried straight through to adulthood. Enter your inner mean girl. Your internal self that negatively challenges everything you say or do, making you second guess your worth at every turn. Your inner mean girl is deep rooted and self-sabotaging and often subconsciously holds us back from healthy relationships, that promotion you really want, that dream job you're trying to land, or starting your own business.

Whatever our goals, our inner mean girl is subtly making us believe that we don't deserve those things. Now you're probably thinking, "Well shit, thanks for the pep talk Kelly, super helpful" but I assure you, you can shut that inner bitch up! Before we dig deep into how to shut our inner mean girl up, I think it's important to realize which areas of our life she is affecting on our path to success. First thing's first, your inner mean girl is not in control of you! Recognizing when she is creeping up is crucial to allow us to flex our boss babe muscles and send her packing!

Fear Can Also Lead Us Into The Depths Of Our Inner Mean Girl And Send Us Running In The Opposite Directions Of Our Goals.

Fear is something we all experience both professionally and personally. I have lived many years in fear. I followed the list of "shoulds" and when I fell flat on my face, I spent years fighting like hell to prove the world wrong. I continued to follow the path of "shoulds", somewhat trying to conform to what I was "supposed to do". I went to school, started a career, had a baby, and a failed relationship resulting in me becoming a single mother; which only pushed me harder to prove the world wrong. I did what I had to do. I enjoyed life, but never truly felt like that was all it had to offer me. My fear of failure allowed my inner mean girl to make me believe that I wasn't able to follow my dreams. What if I fail? What if I don't have enough money to provide for my family? What if I'm not successful? What if people don't support me? What if I don't have time for everything? Will I be able to be everything to my family and my business? These are all very valid worries to have when pursuing a new endeavor, a new business, a new career, etc. However, if we never follow our dreams, will we ever truly find happiness? This was a question I asked myself many times and in the end when my inner mean girl had very little control over me, I decided that my answer was no. No, I would never truly feel like I was able to fulfill my purpose.

Until you begin to challenge your inner mean girl's bitchy little voice, it will always be difficult to face your fears.

Facing your fears is scary as hell but I believe that so is living a life that you don't love. *"What if I fall? Oh but my Darling, what if you fly?"* – *Erin Hanson.* I remember the first time I saw this quote, it resonated so deeply with me. It was the first time I had decided that I believed in my dreams a lot more than I believed in my fears. You are reading this book because you are on your own journey to success, so let me ask you, are your dreams bigger than your fears? What is your "why"? We have a saying in my business, "Your why should make you cry".

For a long time, my why was the obvious choice, I want a better life for my daughter. Now, don't get me wrong, this is very true but I conformed once again to what I "should" say. It wasn't until much later that I realize my true reason for embarking on a life of entrepreneurship was - me. There I said it and I don't even feel bad about it! I am the reason I choose to work my ass off every single day. My work makes me happy, truly happy; it fulfills me in ways I didn't know I needed fulfilment. Following my dreams makes me a better woman and therefore a better mother; imagine that! Your reason for embarking on your journey may be different from mine but please remember that whatever your reasons are, they make you happy, truly happy. And when fear teams up with your inner mean girl, your why needs to be bigger than their power to make you second guess yourself. Believe in yourself babe, you are capable of anything you set your mind to. All those long days, late nights, missed social functions, sweat, and tears are the proof that your hard work will pay off. Your inner mean girl isn't nearly as powerful as your dedication, hard work, passion and belief in yourself. I've talked a lot about believing in yourself, but I think it's important to share that this is a process. Some of you beautiful babes may have always believed you were meant to do big things and that's amazing, but for many of us, that wasn't our reality. I knew that I was able to succeed. But, I knew that I was able to succeed at surviving; surviving at life, surviving at making an income, at providing for my family. But let's be really clear here. Surviving and pursuing a life by design are not the same thing. Not in the least. I can remember the moment I started believing in myself, truly believing in my ability to live the life that I wanted. It was late on a Sunday night and I was working away (as usual), and I sat back and looked at the work I had just produced and thought, "I can really do this", "I actually AM capable of this". For the first time in a very long time, I saw what I was capable of. It was a pivotal moment in my career, but more importantly, in my life. It changed me. I was highly motivated to keep going on my path to success, but before I knew it, I was changing my life. Soon, I was removing people from my world who didn't provide joy or support, not letting other people's opinions of my work and my life affect me, being grateful at every turn, and I began to take risks when opportunities presented themselves. I was free! Free from my mean girl. Free from conformity. Free to be happy.

Creating Change Exercise

I want you to consider where you are in life right now. Make a list. On the left side, I want you to write down who or what is holding you back. On the right side, I want you to write down who or what is motivating you to keep pushing towards your dreams? Once you have finished this exercise, do some reflecting on what your list has shown you. Consider any changes you need to make to ensure that you are on a healthy path to success and happiness. If your list is longer on the left, please don't panic! Remember that you are the only one who is in control of your happiness and success!

Life and success is a journey. It has its ups and downs, days that are more challenging than others, days that are easier than others. Fear is powerful. Your inner mean girl is powerful. But let's be serious, you are way more powerful! You are in control! You have the power inside of you to believe in yourself, your dreams, your ability, your worth and achieve success in all that you do! Challenging your negative thought patterns (aka your mean girl) is like working a specific muscle group. It takes practice, consistency and dedication. The more you do it, the stronger you become. Changing your mindset and working your ass off will never fail you.

Even if things don't work out the way you hoped, being a badass babe will allow you to view these situations as opportunities for growth versus failures.

Others Do Not Have It Easier, They Just Have It Differently.

When I first started my business, I can remember having overwhelming feelings of jealousy when watching other's succeed. I'm all about girl power, so this was quite difficult for me to understand. The more I recognized these jealous feelings, I was able to realize that I was spending far too much energy comparing myself to others. Comparison is not a bad thing as long as it motivates you and your journey. However, during that time, comparing myself to others allowed my inner mean girl to fuel her fire by implanting negative thoughts about how I wasn't good enough, how I would never be that successful, causing me to feel bitter towards these amazingly hard working and successful people. Let me be clear, I am not perfect and I still have moments when I find myself thinking, "Ugh why is she doing so well at that but it's not going well for me?!?", but as soon as I recognize it is happening, I shut that inner mean girl down so quickly! I use those "Ugh" feelings as motivation. I compliment that person's success and if we have a relationship, I will reach out and ask for tips and guidance about what is working for her. That saying "Keeping up with the Jones" (or in our generation the Kardashians) stands true in the arena of pursuing success as well. There are many people who will knock anyone down to get where they are going, but not you sister! You are better than that! You are gracious and all about empowerment! Stop comparing your beginning to someone else's middle. Comparing your success to another person's success is not helpful. At least it isn't for me. It takes me back to the days where I struggled to believe in myself. It takes me back to an unhealthy place when I would have listened to my mean girl and not taken risks to pursue my happiness.

Do you get caught in the comparison cycle? If so, I want you to stop and take a step back from the situation. This is a time for self-reflection. What is going on in your life? What is happening within your journey? Once you are able to understand what is happening within yourself, you are able to understand your feelings of envy and create a plan of action to propel you back to your vision and your goals.

During times of comparison, I reflect and when I do, I usually realize that I have not been working with as much passion as I normally do. My feelings of jealousy and envy often are a direct reflection on myself and my difficulties at that time. This is hard for me to put out there because I want everyone to believe that I work my ass off all the time, and I do, but I am human. I have days where life takes over and I start taking shortcuts. Then I have to do some serious self-reflection which usually results in a revamped schedule (tip: Making lists and schedules are helpful to show that all things are possible). During self-reflection, I have to do something that used to be incredibly difficult, I have to be vulnerable. I have to be vulnerable with myself and others.

"Vulnerability Is The Birthplace Of Innovation, Creativity And Change" – Brene Brown.

Vulnerability is such an important part of the journey. Being vulnerable is not something any of us are comfortable with, however vulnerability is the foundation of our success. It is the foundation of your truths, hopes, dreams, relationships and growth. It is where your inner mean girl begins and it is also where your mean girl ends. Opening up and putting ourselves out there, is hard as hell. It is hard to put your mind, heart, and vision out into the world and sit back and wait for someone to love or hate what you've created. And although it usually lands somewhere in between the extremes, the minute you open yourself up, your mean girl begins to scream as loud as she can. When this happens, we think of every possible disastrous situation that could (but likely would never) occur. However, something beautiful happens when we are vulnerable, we show our true selves. And in my experience, incredible things happen when people see our true selves. People begin to see us as real women and relate to us. That is where the magic happens and where success is made. When we inspire others to be their best beautiful selves, that is power.

I Believe In You And It Is Time You Believe In Yourself.

No matter what journey you are on, what part of your journey you are in, know that you are able to do whatever you desire. Being a powerful, determined, successful woman is not always easy, but it is always worth it. Your inner mean girl only holds power if you let her. Fear only holds you back when you let it. Shut that bitch up by flexing your bossbabe muscles and show her what you are capable of! Believe in your strength, worth, capabilities, dreams, and ability to succeed. Your desire to succeed must be greater than your fear. Keep your vision clear and remind yourself regularly why you are on this journey. Take time daily to reflect on your goals, it will give you the opportunity to be grateful for the journey; to be grateful for the opportunity to pursue your dreams. When we take the time to be grateful and self-reflect, we take the time to recharge, allowing us to stay motivated and true to our goals. Keep going girl, you got this! For more tips, tricks and badass strategies to breaking up with your inner mean girl, reach out and let's chat; kelly.rolfe@gmail.com. I can't wait to hear from you!

Chapter 3

The Art Of Letting Go – Gracefully, Kindly And Soulfully

by Tania Jane Moraes-Vaz

"In life, we are often faced with choices that will shape us and define us. However, it is not those choices that have a long lasting impact on us and those around us, rather our commitment to them, and our willingness to hold on or let go."
~ Tania Jane Moraes-Vaz

Tania Jane Moraes-Vaz

When asked to sum up her life mantra into a sentence, Tania Jane Moraes-Vaz says that, "Passion always propels change, and kindness always heals everything". And true to this, she leads and coaches those in her interactions and businesses with this motto in mind.

A graduate from the University of Waterloo, majoring in English Literature, Tania is a tenacious, optimistic, passionate, and eclectic lifestyle photographer, writer and creative maven, who enjoys capturing moments – be it through the lens of her camera, or writing on her website, or a notebook when she's on the go. Little did she know that it would be her saving grace through life's challenges, as well as a medium for celebration.

Over the last few years, both photography and writing has evolved into a platform for Tania to spread awareness and empower women and their families about leading a holistically healthy lifestyle, especially after she was diagnosed with PCOS (Polycystic Ovarian Syndrome) 4 years ago. Her fierce and positive attitude has helped her overcome the socio-cultural challenges that she was struggling with emotionally, mentally and physically, all while relearning and creating a whole new lifestyle for herself built on the foundation of being passionate about wanting change for oneself and kindness towards oneself first, on a holistic level. Tania lives in incredible Ontario with her amazing husband and mischievous son.

fb: facebook.com/fleetingmomentsbyjane | t: @taniajmoraesvaz
ig: @fleetingmomentsbyjane | @lifeofanarbonnista | @taniajanemoraesvaz

No is a sentence. Trust me. It has just as much value as a Yes.

Goethe once said that, "Things that matter most must never be at the mercy of the things that matter least". Learning how to say NO, and actually meaning it, while still being kind, has been one of the hardest lessons for me to learn, and implement in all aspects of my life. Establishing healthy boundaries, and choosing ourselves first is not an option, it is a necessity. If we fail to identify when those lines are crossed, the outcomes manifest themselves holistically – on an emotional, mental and physical level.

Each choice and commitment carries with it a certain kind of energy; an aura, a feeling. We may feel a burning and positive desire to really help a person, take on a project, or put ourselves in an environment or situation that has a positive influence on us. However, sometimes there are choices and commitments that are asked of us that may make us feel anxious, and uncomfortable; but we still say yes to them perhaps out of obligation, sympathy, relationship ties/history, and only in hindsight do we realize that we had a choice - The choice to decline the job offer or project that did not resonate with our soul, or knowing when to bow out gracefully but yet firmly out of a relationship – be it a significant other, family or friendship only because we are burning ourselves out by offering too much of ourselves, without being appreciated for it. We are always going to be presented with choices that either demand a burning and elated YES within us, or elicit a firm and resolute NO, despite how hard it may be to actually stand one's ground. Our commitment to these choices is what makes them have a positive or negative impact in our lives – be it our commitment to a person, place or situation – towards each other, and most of all, towards ourselves. We all have within us the ability to choose what is best for ourselves, however, we need to exercise that muscle on a daily basis.

Four years ago, I was rushed to the ER at the local hospital due to a stabbing pain in my lower left abdomen. Fast forward 11 hours later, it was diagnosed that I had a twisted left ovary, with ovarian cysts and an emergency surgery would be required. The next day, while in recovery, my OB-GYN let me know that I have Polycystic Ovarian Syndrome which affects 1 in 10 women. He mentioned that this is a health condition caused by hormonal imbalances and is a leading cause of infertility if not managed properly with various medication, diet and exercise. At 23 years old, I was told that I may or may not be able to have children at any given point in my life. I was heartbroken, and confused as to how and why this event occurred in my life. I felt as though my choice to have children was taken away from me before I had even met the right person to build a life with. Hence, during my recovery period from surgery, I started to look into natural cures and ways to manage my symptoms and really address the root cause of PCOS, which is multifactorial, and of course I wanted to manage and treat this as naturally as possible.

Through this research, I came across my naturopath, and acupuncturist for treatment, wherein I was forced to really examine the quality of my life on a holistic level. Something they asked me during my initial visit ended up as recurring questions through the last few years: How am I managing my stress levels? What are the sources of my stress? Can I work on prioritizing myself first by eliminating my sources of stress on a gradual basis? Stressors can be environmental, physical, fiscal, emotional, relational. It was in reflecting on these questions that I had my eureka moment - The month I ended up in the hospital for emergency surgery was also when my stress levels were at an all-time high – financially, emotionally, mentally and physically. I was constantly overworking myself in order to escape certain emotional stressors at home, and of course looking for a way to somehow manage my life, but failing miserably at it. Why? Because I simply couldn't muster up the courage to say NO, or politely decline whatever social, volunteer, financial and family commitments that came my way –

especially when they didn't feel too good on a soulful level. Little did I realize that my body and soul were telling me that I was being unkind to myself while being kind and overextending myself to everyone around me.

The underlying message was that in order to heal myself internally and externally:

- I had to work on identifying and eliminating any and all forms of stress that were impacting me negatively – toxic situations, habits, and relationships.

- For once, I had to learn to be kind and brave towards myself, and stand up for myself. I viewed this as a chance to design a life that I actually wanted to no longer escape from. I wanted to face my stressors one day at a time and have the courage to view them for what they were and say, "No thank you, I choose myself this time – my time, happiness, and most of all, my wellbeing", and slowly but surely, things in my life began aligning themselves accordingly.

Your NO has just as much power as your YES - these two statements are your personal currency which enable you to choose whom and what you allow into your life or not. And when you exercise this power with respect for yourself first, those around you will come to respect you, and the boundaries that you establish.

Establish Boundaries And Do Not Be Apologetic For It.

Once we are aware of what needs to change, and we start seeking these positive changes in our lives, we will see situations, and people for what they really are, instead of the rose-colored, idealized versions we fall for in our mind and heart. Too often, we may feel that just because we have known someone for a long time, or because they may be related to us, we need to let things go. We let their negatively impacting behavior slide by, giving them the benefit of the doubt or making excuses for their behavior. One doesn't have to be a bad person to have negative behaviors, however, there is a fine line between focusing on the positive aspects of a person, versus their consistently negative behavior that does not seem to change, no matter how many times you may have tried to discuss it with them, or the chances you may have given them.

One such instance was when I had to let go of a really close friendship last year. We had known each other for ten years, and had been there for each other through everything respectively. However last year, during both our wedding planning processes, we reached an impasse in our friendship, whereby I had overextended and overexerted myself in trying to be there for her in the best possible ways during her wedding planning process, which negatively impacted me personally, professionally and emotionally as well. Meanwhile the same was not reciprocated towards me, and she never really saw how her behavioral patterns impacted me, and made me feel throughout the year. I had let this situation get out of control and I was afraid to tell her how I truly felt, that I felt anxious and resentful every time I was around her, or we spoke, and this negativity started to consume me. Before coming to the decision that I needed to let go of this friendship, I had to really reflect on our relationship dynamic, and noticed that this person had certain behaviors that were definitely not going to change, and as such, our friendship took on more of a forced effort to maintain over the years. I realized that I held onto it so tightly due to the years and emotion invested in this friendship. This is when I knew I had to tell her how I felt, even if it meant losing the friendship. When I finally approached her to discuss how I felt, and establish boundaries, it did not sit well with her, as I asked her to step down from the bridal party, which was by far the hardest thing for me to do.

Was it easy to have this conversation with someone you have

shared some of your fondest memories, and most vulnerable moments with? NO. Was it necessary to stand up for myself, and take back my personal power? YES. I realized that these behaviors kept recurring since I kept allowing it by constantly putting up with it, and not being honest with myself and with the opposite person about how I truly felt. I let go of this relationship with a positive heart and mind, and with respect for the memories that were shared and built over the years. I finally felt free, like a weight had been lifted off myself - all because I mustered up the courage to view a behavior for what it was, and take a stand against it.

Any relationship, be it with your significant other, friends, or even family, needs to be founded not on a 50/50 ratio, but a 100/100 and the extra mile basis, especially if these individuals say they love you and care for you, and moreover if they have a vested interest in your wellbeing.

Stop Questioning Your Gut Instinct; Instead, Lean In To It.

I mentioned earlier that each individual, commitment and choice carries a certain type of energy with it. One such way to identify it is by becoming attuned to your own energy levels, and also that which you encounter – individual or situation. I believe in trusting your gut instinct and the vibe you get from any person or place. Energy never lies. Notice how you feel when you are around positive vs. negative energy. Notice your body's response, pay attention to it. Your body is often most in tune with the energy it encounters, before the mind even wants to accept it. Observe how you feel when you are around a certain place, conversation or person or even after your interactions – It is your body telling you to pick up on the energy of that person, place or situation. Be it sincere and positive, or malicious and insincere, you will always know it and feel it. Whenever I have ignored my instincts is when I have suffered my biggest regrets, and betrayals; whereas, whenever I have paid attention to it is when I have been rewarded with a strong sense of peace and calm.

Identify Your Top 10 Priorities & Choose Your 5 Non-Negotiable Commitments.

The ability to say NO, and to be kind to yourself, comes with an awareness of what is it that makes you feel inherently good, and ultimately an awareness of how you want to feel when you take on a certain commitment. It's not just about what looks good on the outside, but also what feels like complete bliss to your heart and soul.

For instance, earlier this year, I left my adrenaline pumping -high stress - great perks - not to mention an amazing team – corporate finance role in order to further better my health holistically, since I definitely did not want to impact it again. Work was not exactly going well, but I was idealistic and trying to make the best of my situation. I was looking forward to my Christmas vacation to have some time off to disconnect and relax. Apart from spending time with loved ones, I reflected upon the quality of my life, and where it was headed. Let me tell you, the life I envisioned for myself and my family was nowhere close to what it actually was. The sad reality was that I was constantly pushing myself to do things to the point of burnout, that I had no time for myself, my health, or my loved ones. I was too tired to enjoy a nice meal on weeknights and the weekends were spent recuperating in bed for the most part, and not doing things I enjoyed, be it catching up with friends, going to a yoga class, or even going out on a date night with my spouse. I felt that my life was a giant blur of days and nights where I was operating mindlessly. I knew something needed to change, as I was running on empty, and it was a matter of time before I crashed and burned. My heart knew what I needed to do, yet my mind was unwilling to accept that and it was a tough decision to come to. Leaving was bittersweet since I had formed some great relationships, but it was a cathartic experience since I finally felt like I gained my soul back. I finally launched my photography business that I had been putting off, started a new health and wellness business in my time off, and I also ended up finding a new role in a different industry much closer to home, with a firm that had tremendous respect for pursuing work-life balance. Taking a stand for what truly makes you feel good won't be easy, however, focus on how you want to feel, and the outcome will align itself accordingly.

Who's Your Tribe? Distinguish Unconditional Support Vs. Unnecessary Sabotage.

When creating positive change for ourselves, it is hard to let go of something altogether, but it is even harder to stand your ground and conserve your energy when faced with a person, situation or choice that you may not necessarily have the opportunity to get away from completely. In these times, it's important to have a support system of people who are completely in your corner and can support you by stepping up and saying no on your behalf while you are still learning how to do so and remind you of your WHY. To me, these were my significant other, and my best friends.

While being treated for PCOS, in addition to the emotional and physical fitness component, was a dietary requirement to cut out all forms of sugar, dairy and gluten from my diet. I'll be the first to admit that cutting out sugar from my diet felt as though someone asked me to never have water again. However, I slowly overcame these challenges and managed to stay true to my commitment to myself and my health, and the big picture of having a family someday, thanks to the help of my significant other. Meanwhile, my own family never really understood why I could no longer eat the way they all did, or that their years of unnecessary emotional badgering was unhealthy, and had a very visible impact on me even after having a sit down discussion with them regarding my health and the consequences I'd likely be facing if I did not give this my whole hearted effort. In most gatherings with friends or family, my significant other was always in my corner, encouraging me, and reminding me of my WHY – why I needed to respect my commitment to myself holistically – whether it meant staying strict with my diet, or getting myself to destress by taking time to myself and not overcommitting to people or situations that never made me feel good to begin with, or even just staying physically fit or even slowly limiting how much I associate with certain individuals who were emotionally draining – be it friends or family. Fast forward four years later, I have slowly gathered the strength and courage to say NO to table full of sinfully delicious but not Tania-friendly food, overloaded weeks that completely drain me, and anything that makes me feel as though I am not enough. My support system, and most of all the awareness of what it was that I needed to do to heal internally and externally, is how we were blessed by our son this year, when in fact four years ago, I was given a diagnosis of having a slim chance of being able to conceive naturally.

Learning to let go of what impacts oneself negatively is not an easy feat – one only gets stronger every time they utilize this power muscle. This does not mean that my journey of healing and growth ends here; rather it's an ongoing process which requires me to stay consistently respectful and kind to myself first, enabling me to be respectful and kind towards those I love. Only when you are able to be whole to yourself, and commit to what resonates most with how you want to feel and live, that you will be able to let go what is unhealthy for yourself in any facet of your life.

Chapter 4

The Inner Workings Of External Influences

by Karina K Ullrich

Don't let people pull you into their storm, pull them into your peace.
~ Kimberly Jones

Karina K Ullrich

Karina is a visionary entrepreneur who specializing in the development of basic daily essentials that are functionally superior, environmentally clean and with an all-natural aesthetic. She and her husband are the founders of Evolatree.com. Together, they're paving the way to a future full of sustainable products that will reduce waste in the landfills. It all started back in 2010 while living in China, she became attracted to the lure of traditional Chinese medicine. With a background in hairdressing, she honed in on the uniqueness of the wood combs that were superior in quality and culturally unique. She set out to share with the world the origins of the comb and to bring about its use into daily rituals once again. The first holiday season in sales was but a shoebox full of combs. The business was just a hobby when they had decided to move back home to Canada. With full intention of needing part time jobs to make it, perseverance and drive proved otherwise. Karina and her husband have successfully lived off the fruit of their efforts from that time forward. Since then, the evolatree line has expanded to include bamboo boxer briefs and natural fiber sunglasses.

Karina is a manufacturing director for new entrepreneurs who are seeking production for their sustainable designs as well as sourcing manufacturers with new and trending ecofriendly products for emerging businesses. She can show you that business can be done ethically and be environmentally friendly and yet also profitable. By simply influencing one entrepreneur, a whole community can be positively affected.

fb: facebook.com/evolatree | ig: @evolatree
karina@evolatree.com | www.evolatree.com

INFLUENCES ARE ALL around us in a multitude of forms. Often, these take shape in objects, places or thoughts, but how often do we consider the ones we live and work with or the people in our social circles? How people affect your success in life comes down to the lifestyle we choose to lead. Is it possible to make a difference in yourself if the people around you aren't similarly doing the same? The ones we surround ourselves with can leave an impact the size of a crater if left unchecked. Would it be easier to succeed if the ones around you were doing equally as well? Strategically use people to leverage your success and find strength in social circles. Throughout my life and in my business, I have found that the influential stress people pose on us can be detrimental to our success and can be avoided if we incorporate solutions into our daily habits. Once we perfect those habits, success becomes easy. I have come to realize that if you don't design your own life plan, you may end up mingling with the wrong tribe, enabling others to do it for you. For myself, I've always been clear in my vision of the lifestyle I want to lead. I've always been focused and kept myself on path towards this vision. It's easy to become functional and happy when you aren't stuck on other people's stresses. Imagine a time when you felt limited, you know you're growing but just can't make it to the level that you aimed to be. It is possible to grow stagnant in an environment, for myself I found this to be true. Since coming to these conclusions, I've learned to differentiate between the people that can positively affect my happiness and success vs. the ones that stumble my stride.

Build An Empire Through Making A Difference In Yourself.

It's important to have someone to talk to, someone to brainstorm ideas with. This person may or may not be involved in your business at all, however, they contribute their listening ear, constructive advice, helpful suggestions for goals and plans for executing them. The ones we surround ourselves with will be the pillars to our success. Back when I was dating my husband, I had very specific criteria for his role in my life. He would be someone whose goals are consistent with mine. A strategic alliance is what makes a win or a loose in the partnership of life. Does his lifestyle reflect that of positive habits? Do his words embody motivation and support? Do I feel encouraged to fulfill my dreams? This support can come from anyone connected to your home or professional life, such as a friend, spouse, partner, or family member. This person should be a constant in your life, your steady rock who is consistently present. Whoever this person is, getting in the habit of having a daily pow-wow with them can improve your focus and determination. This quick and simple daily conference can be highly motivating and keep up the momentum of pursuing your goals and dreams. Even if you're doing all the talking, it's enough to bring about reality to your thoughts; to speak them is the first act in creating them. This daily ritual can be broken into several minds with the same principle. For example, I often speak with my husband to divulge my thoughts, but I also seek insight from my dad and other family members as well. Home is where the heart is. It's the foundation from which it grows. My habits can ultimately lead to a successful life. My home life and habits therein will be a mirror image; a reflection of the day I embark upon. These are the elements that affect your ability to build an empire.

The Fabric Of Life.

Much like the role that the people in our home life fulfill, our friends, workmates and neighbors will also help weave the fabric to success in life. Have you ever been consumed by the stress accumulated simply by being around someone else' problems? Have you ever missed out on opportunities due to aiding in someone else' affairs? Be sure not to let other people's stress become your stress. A toxic person will continually unload their problems onto you. Try to disengage these people by offering help in ways that are suitable to you, rather than succumbing to their demands. Keep the ball in your court. Maintain control by setting guidelines for yourself. Once you establish the rules you live by, the commitment you give to serve others is easily definable. I can often be a people pleaser; I simply loved seeing the enjoyment I could bring about in a person. Although this is a remarkable gift to give someone, I learned that I must put myself first and foremost. Even if you feel guilty for not providing that soft cushion landing for that person when they need it the most, have the courage to stand up for yourself. When you place your own wellbeing above all others, you're actually contributing to more than just yourself, you are ensuring that you're functionally sound and prepared to handle whatever or whomever the world throws at you. I have found solace in surrounding myself with people who walk to the rhythm of my beat.

Once you find those kin alike to your heart, incorporate them into every aspect of your life. Within work and through play and every day in between, include these people every step of the way. I am all too aware of how difficult it can be to evade the persuasion of friends and those you hang around with in free time. Free time isn't exactly what it seems and is quite the opposite in actuality. If your free time involves completely averting from your day-to-day achievements, how is that serving you? The time we spend with ourselves and with others should always be fulfilling some aspect of our dreams and ambitions. How do we do this? Weave work and lifestyle together. When I was a kid, my dad would always tell me to choose a career path that had a lifestyle I wanted to live. This is imperative. I don't live a life that I need to take a vacation from. My vacations are incorporated into my work life. My spare time is spent doing things that contribute to paint the grand portrait of my life.

Do your friends or family believe in you? Do they take you seriously when you say you have to work? When your job doesn't consist of the regular 9-5, clock in and clock out work life, people seldom consider self-employed work a 'job' and assume that you are in complete control and have the ability to manipulate timetables accordingly. It's true you do have the power to create your own timetable; however, being in control of your work schedule requires you to be strict with yourself and others. Being self-employed and having a warehouse all to my husband and myself is awesome. We've grown it to resemble some of the comforts from home with the functionality of an office. We spend all our time there. It's amazing; however, setting working hours is a line that often gets blurred. All too often, we find ourselves conforming to other people's demands. I began to ask myself if this person made me feel good. Did I feel good about what they're asking of me? Whether it's a coworker, friend or family member, be sure to put your business and your own wellbeing first.

The Art Of Listening.

Being on the receiving end of a lack of discernment from the ones we serve can be frustrating and leave us troubled with how to deal with the situation. All too often, comments can be taken personally which can make it difficult to resolve the matter without letting feelings shine through like they always do. In my ecommerce business, I often deal with customer requests and comments. However unreasonable their questions, comments or concerns may be, it is miraculously efficient to handle their situations with a 'no sweat' demeanor. Ultimately, their problems aren't problems unless I respond with the same fiery fuel that ignited the situation in the first place. However rude you may perceive someone's actions to be, it is 100% how you respond that sets the tone for the outcome and resolution.

Is it your job to win people over?
Absolutely not.

The only thing you can do is listen to them, share facts and apply all the resources you're able to offer.

If a customer has a neutral or lesser comment to reflect upon your product or service, disregard it as being anecdotal. Take no personal offence to the words of others. Their voice cannot effect positive change unless it is uplifting or genuinely thought through; full of insight and wisdom. All criticism can be taken in openly but should be catalogued according to relevance. Sometimes these are often personal biases and are not constructive. Sometimes, it's not worth your efforts. For example, I deal with this in my product development business due to the fact that our product manufacture is outsourced overseas. There is a stereotype attached to the made in – insert country – labeling. Stereotypes are often generated from a misinformed or uneducated opinion of something, so it can bring about an opportunity to share knowledge about your industry. For instance, many of our products are manufactured overseas, which doesn't usually receive much positive interest until I exclaim we travel abroad ourselves and work with small run manufacturers to produce our goods. We also follow fair trade practices; quality and ethics are very important to us. However, even still, we often stumble upon the "I don't like anything made in China" fear based conjecture. In the early days of our business, this misinformed mindset would stump me and I would stress about having to explain myself with those types because they will seldom listen to my story once so deep in their version of reality. I learned to overcome this recurring issue by giving zero attention to these individuals and letting them walk away. Instead I'd focus on the open minded ones, and give them my full energy. I love talking about my business; I love telling my story. I love engaging in a conversation with a truly open-minded person and divulging all my wondrous secrets of the world I know and just how magnificent and environmentally focused we are trying to be with our products. I stopped trying to win over the people that would in turn just drain my energy.

I learned to acknowledge them, listen to
them and disengage by letting
them walk away.

It was a highly effective method for both parties because often the person standing in front of me simply only wanted to be heard. It was my respect for them that enabled me to detach any personal offence from the scenario. By doing this, my response grew more attention from these individuals; once I gave them my listening ear, they all the same gave me theirs. I created the perfect environment for successful transaction.

When you're in business, nearly 50% of the people you encounter are also people in business. It is incredibly easy to leverage your business by surrounding yourself with these gems. They are the ones from whom you will learn, share ideas with and receive support. Listening is an essential tool to master. Avoid over speaking; people want to be heard. There is a wealth of answers residing in the words others feed you. Use this information to formulate specific, targeted responses that will bring about the resolution to all those with queries you encounter.

*"The biggest communication problem is we do not
listen to understand. We listen to reply."*
~ Unknown

The Only Thing Holding You Back Is Not Moving Forward.

Invest in yourself by carefully selecting the ones you commune with. Make lifestyle changes and cultivate a routine where you're actively communicating your passions to others. Make them known to the world and have confidence that your pursuits will stand the test of your efforts. Avoid succumbing to the undesirable needs of others by maintaining a set of guidelines for yourself. We can learn through the act of teaching itself. Place yourself in a position where you are actively showing others the map to leading a healthy lifestyle. I've come to understand that the packaging is everything; you're the package. The product does not represent you, nor does the service you provide. People are buying the package; your story, it's what you stand for that counts. Listen to and take note of your surroundings. Stress is an illusion, it can be transformed, and you can take it and will it into a source of power. Handle stress like water beading off the duck. You got this.

Section 2

Family Matters:
Thriving Through It All

featuring

Stephanie Butler, Eva Macias, Sunit Suchdev, and Kathryn Yeatman

Editorial commentary by Ky-Lee Hanson

THERE ARE MANY ways one could feel lost in life. It is very easy to get wrapped up in the day to day aspects of society and it's easy to put other's needs before our own. Priorities come with a lot of pressure. For many of us, there is career, business, bosses, clients, kids, spouse, friends, finances, society, health, bill collectors, home maintenance and so much more pulling us in every direction. We could also find ourselves wrapped up in someone else's dream and we may have stopped paving the way towards our own. We may also not know what that dream of ours is.

If you find yourself buried under other people's problems, or goals, or maybe you are buried under a pile of your own work, whatever the case may be, a big help can be analyzing your relationship with time. Finding time for yourself and for self-reflection. Look at your life from an outside perspective, do you recognize yourself? Where are you headed?

Balancing life and staying on top of priorities requires skill. It is work to create systems but once they are in place and habit is created, the stress of being neck deep in chaos may not seem so bad. I am the farthest thing from an organized person, but once I took control of where I am headed, the boulders being thrown at me just became a part of the routine. I accept them and know more are coming. I am not going to get stuck under them. They will get dealt with but I do not give them or anyone else, my power.

The attitude I now have because I do not let life's priorities put pressure on me, and my relationship with time is a reasonable one. You will hear me say in stressful situations, "Ok, I understand this needs to be dealt with. I have time tomorrow. I am not going to stress about the what-ifs, we will deal with that if it happens. As of now, that isn't reality."

It's never that we are too busy, it is that we prioritize something else more or have not taken the time to sit down to see the value of abundance. Have you heard before, "Are your priorities in check?"

A great way to think is, "What CAN I do to make this happen" instead of, "I DON'T have time" or, "I CAN'T afford it". We may not be perfect, we don't know it all, but we do need to put effort into changing our lives and growing aka LIVING. Our words create our belief system and our belief becomes our reality. What we need to start owning is our capability which most people sell themselves short on.

I am always amazed at the women I call partners and coauthors of mine. They run full time businesses, households, stay healthy and also plan things like weddings, write books with me, start up charities, are going through surgery, family loss, and / or so much more. Do I hear them make excuses or complain? Honestly, never. Sure we make jokes and are crazy, like, 80% of the time, but we are so full of life because we make it abundant, not busy. When there is will, there is way.

The common trait I see in my clients, partners and coauthors as well as in my mentors, is that they see themselves as a priority. They do not live their life exclusively for someone or something else. They have done what is necessary to grab control of their happiness and dreams. When they are happy and flourishing, so is the world around them. Women are strong, we are the givers of life and the dominant nurturing role. Stephanie Butler, Eva Macias, Sunit Suchdev and Kathryn Yeatman help us to explore if we are not happy, healthy, excited, flourishing and nurtured, how can we expect ourselves to be capable of doing that for others?

We each deserve to be the main character
in our own story.

Chapter 5

Organize Your Life

by Stephanie Butler

Being organized isn't about getting rid of everything you own or trying to become a different person; it's about living the way you want to live, but better. ~ Andrew Mellen

Stephanie Butler

Stephanie was born and raised in the north end of Toronto, Ontario and now lives in Barrie, Ontario where she loves the small city feel to it; yet she is a short distance to hiking trails and the lake. Stephanie spent her summers in the Kawartha's; camping, swimming, building forts, fishing and around camp fires. Her time up north was one of good friendships and a sense of community, and she had freedom to explore and learn who she was. She still visits every year.

Stephanie has a background in social service work, 20 years in the mental health field, and has a flare for working with people who have depression, ADD and emotional attachment to their belongings. She feels it is an honor to be able to support people along in their journey. Being a professional organizer has been a lifelong dream for Stephanie; she loves what she does and feels blessed to help others in this very unique way.

Being in business for herself, she chooses where she will spend her time in the community, supporting different causes. She donates her time, services and monies wherever she can, but mainly supports Youth Mental Health, Lupus and other local businesses. Her dream is to be a philanthropist.

fb: facebook.com/SerenityOrganizingSolutionswithStephanie

www.serenityorganizingsolutions.ca

AS I HAVE quoted Andrew Mellen above, I want to emphasize as a professional organizer that I do not want people to get rid of all their belongings, have rigid schedules and live in a stark environment. I sometimes get the feeling that this is how we can be perceived. My main goal as an organizer is to create a cozy, functional and serene space for my clients. My job is to hear what my client's goals are for their lifestyle, then organize and help them reduce their items to meet their objectives by the end of our time together. I help people to lower their internal stressors through ways they have control to do so.

For 20 years, I was in the mental health field and worked as a case manager. I loved working with people and found it to be such a blessing for them to let me become part of their journey toward recovery and growth. We all live in a world where there are always going to be outside stressors: bills, sickness, relationships, work and so on. What I supported people to do was to make healthy choices to make their lives healthier through working with doctors, therapists, getting affordable housing, working on their budget, addressing where they could have control of what they were doing in their life. The underlying theme was the internal stressors that caused people more stress than the external ones; that voice in our head that tells us we are not good enough, we are doing it all wrong, we have to please everyone … etc. Working with others helped me to work on my own internal stressors and made me want to share what I have learned.

As I mentioned before, I love working with people, they are what makes me excited in life; seeing them grow, reach their goals and keep on dreaming big. I took the tools I learned in the social work field and have been able to use it in my professional organizing business. Clutter usually isn't just about clutter. What are the underlying issues: perfectionism, fear, too much on one's plate, not all family members are on the same page? Whatever the issue is, there is a way to address it and make changes.

It has been said that what one's desk/house looks like is a reflection of their mind. If we live in clutter, we have stress. We waste time looking for things, we create anxiety that we have lost something, it is on the back of our mind that we need to clean that junk drawer or spare room, we have shame about having clutter, our lives feel closed in because we do not have room to stretch out, literally.

Through decluttering, purging items and organizing all items in your home, it provides a sense of calm because you know where everything is and can find it easily, you can tidy up quickly since you know where everything goes and you have room to move around. We have control over our space and when our space is in order, we lower our stress and become more productive in the areas we want to spend our time on.

I have worked with many different families and have seen many things, but there are a few re-occurring issues that come up; the main one is not having enough time. I have come up with a system to tackle this daily adventure and I believe that anyone can adopt it to fit into their lifestyle. My system is easy and done in four steps.

TIME, That 4 Letter Word

I think we all wish we could add more hours to the day in order to complete all we want to get done. The problem with this way of thinking is that everything is so important we have to get it done now! We live in a society that applauds overworking and spending copious amounts of hours being busy. I would like to challenge everyone to think the complete opposite. We do not need to get everything done now and we should work on "being" instead of "doing". I spent years running from one unfinished project to the next and never feeling satisfied or a sense of accomplishment. I was scrambling to get my list of tasks done on a daily basis but always seemed to fall short. All this negativity had me riddled with anxiety and I was stressed to the max. I would wake in the morning, look at my to do list and want to curl back into bed as it seemed hopeless to make a dent in it and I had no clue where to start. I knew I couldn't be the only one feeling this way and living in a loop of insanity, trying to be perfect at it. I came to a point where I was sick and tired of finding myself in the exact same spot; needing more time to accomplish all my tasks and being busy all the time. I was exhausted.

I read several books and spoke to many people about how they seem to "have it all together" and I made my own system to create more time for myself; No, I am not a witch and I cannot create time out of thin air, but I can create more time by using it more wisely and efficiently.

TIME Is A 4 Step Process To Keep One On Track And Focused On What Is Important

T= To do list, create one for work, for home and for any other obligations (volunteer work). Make the list clear and to the point.

I = Itemize list in priority: rank each item with a 1, 2 or 3. 1 is something that is due in the next day or so. 2 is something you need complete in about a weeks' time and 3 is something you don't need to do right away, may be able to delegate or something you no longer deem important. We can always re-evaluate our lists and change our minds as to what we truly consider to be aligned with our goals and to be sure to use our time wisely.

M = Map out how long each task will take to complete; you may need to break tasks down into smaller tasks. Now schedule each task into your agenda based on its due date. We can have fabulous to do list's but the odds of us keeping it on track and completing things on time is very rare if we do not schedule the time to do so. I used to pick all the easy things on my "to do list", get them done and put off the tougher stuff where I would tackle on a totally random basis, whenever I found myself with extra time. When does that ever happen? I would then rewrite my list and add some new things to it and so on and so on. I would keep seeing the same tasks from week to week and not getting it done. This caused stress and anxiety for me, so I implemented this system.

E = Execute on a daily basis. If I schedule my tasks into my agenda, then I will be working toward my goals daily and will see how much closer I am getting toward completing my dreams. This gives me a sense of pride, accomplishment and a sense of control. Much better than feeling hopeless, tired and stressed all the time.

I usually use TIME on Monday mornings to map out my week ahead and keep me on track for the following weeks. Remember our "to do lists" can be fluid, so we can change our mind on commitments we once said yes to. We have a right to change our mind if it truly interferes with our value system and our main goals. Why spend time on something that is not generating you money, bringing your family closer together or supporting your community to be the best it can be?

How To Organize The Family's TIME

When using TIME with family obligations, it can get a bit busy keeping track of everyone's schedules. This is where a Family Command Centre (FCC) can be used in your household, usually set up in the kitchen. A FCC is unique to each household depending on what style works best for you and how it looks. Check out Pinterest for beautiful ideas. Most FCC's have a monthly calendar to mark important appointments for all family members. It has bins or file folders for each family member to hold onto important papers: permission slips for school, event flyers and so forth. It is great to have a chalk or white board to leave message for one another. Another useful tool is "a week at a glance." This is where you can map out the week for everyone's schedules: work hours, skating lessons, date night etc. A lot of families name their FCC using their last name or has everyone's first initial somewhere and so forth. Really make the space represent your family, have fun with it and have everyone contribute to it in some way. The FCC main function is to keep everyone in the family on track of each other's schedules and to take responsibility for connecting with one another when they need to. It teaches children independence, helps with reading and scheduling one's time appropriately. You can always use pictures in the week for younger children to be able to participate, but always label the picture to encourage reading.

Create Time By Saying NO

In the past, I found myself with such a busy, non-stop schedule where I was not able to get things done. The largest lesson is to say no more often. I used to fear saying no, the fear of disappointing others, not looking like I was available or the fear of confrontation. I was taught by a mentor of mine how to say no without actually saying no, by using the following, "Thanks for asking, I will have to check my schedule, when do you need to know by? I will get back to you by that date with my answer." I didn't have to say no and it gives me time to see if this task is aligned with my values, timetable and ultimate goals with work and family. If I do not want to do the task, I let that person know, "I am sorry, but it is not a good fit for me right now." Saying no to more things, allows me to have more time available to work on my goals, dreams and opens up time for new adventures to enter my life. I was approached to write this chapter and I had to give it serious thought: Was it something to help me in my career? Would I have enough time to truly dedicate to it? Does this book represent what I believe in and match my values? The answers were all yes and so I went ahead with this project. I am thrilled to be part of it and could have only had the time since I said no to other projects that were not the right fit for me. When it comes to saying no, we tend to put pressure on ourselves about needing to answer right away. Most questions do not need to be answered right away unless it is a restaurant and the waiter needs your order, and still you can ask for a couple more minutes to look over the menu, so take that stressor off the table. Take all the time you need to see if you have the time to dedicate to it, that it aligns with your values and it is working toward your ultimate goals. I had created time for myself, for this wonderful opportunity by implementing TIME and saying no more often.

Letting Go

Speaking of saying no more often, let's look at holding onto items we no longer need or use. If you are not open to letting go of older items, you will never have enough room to receive new items into your life. If we hold on so tightly to our items, our hands and arms cannot be open to receive new things in our life, and those things are usually what we need to move forward and grow. I need to be out of my comfort zone 90% of the time, this allows me to know I am growing. This pertains to all areas of my life: work, family, relationships, networking, travel, goals etc. I need to always be pushing myself to want more for myself. This is the only way I know to be available for new adventures to enter my life and a place where I can even imagine doing half the things I have already done; Starting a business at 40 years old and saying goodbye to a 20-year career, travelling on my own in the UK/Paris, writing this chapter, taking up painting, kayaking and other activities when I thought I was too old to start and who knows what else is to come. My experience has shown me that the sky is the limit for everyone who is willing to put themselves out there.

When I hold onto the past, I am adding stress to my life, and when I am trying to control the present and the unfolding of the future which I have very little control of, I create fear.

I can have many detailed plans of how
the next opportunity in my life is to go,
but ultimately it will unfold how
it is meant to unfold.

This may seem scary to most but remember we are always taken care of; our needs are always met in every second of every day. Ask yourself, "Right now do I need anything?" The answer will always be no. You have clothes, have shelter, have food to eat and so forth. We are taken care of. With this belief, I do my best to move forward and toward my goals, instead of holding onto what I have as I know the possibilities are endless if one is open to them.

How You Can Create Space In Your Home

I want each of you to try something out; it will create openness to possibilities and will create flow in your life/home. When you bring something new into your home, donate one to two of your belongings. If we have 15 – 20 % of empty space, we are creating room for new things to enter our life. If I donate items to a local shelter, I know they will get a new life and will be used on a regular basis. Items sitting in my home, collecting dust either in a box or on a shelf, deserve to live the life they were made to live. So when inventorying your items, ask yourself, "Do I use this?", "How often do I use it?", "When will I use it next?". If you do not have an answer to these questions, it is time to send that item onto its new journey. Just think of the happiness it will bring to a new person who needs it and will use it. Again, if you hold onto items and let them sit there, you have kept that item from its purpose in life and you have taken up valuable space in your home for new items that can make you happy.

Keep a bag or box in your closet to store items you plan on donating. Once it is full, donate those items.

Another good way to keep a set number of clothing is to only keep a set number of hangers in your closet, once you donate one, you have room for something new.

Why Make These Changes?

By using TIME in our lives, we find we have more time to do the things we want and need to do. If we are open to new adventures and belongings to enter our lives, we will be able to receive them with open arms. To make change happen, we need to make changes in our day to day living. I challenge you to make one change today. Implement TIME into your weekly routine. Over a short period, you will see items from your "to do list" getting done daily and from those positive actions, you are one step closer to your goals. We all deserve to have time to work toward our goals, have time with friends and family and to live out our dreams. We have an easy time saying no to ourselves all the time. Here is the next challenge: start saying no to the outside world more often. Why waste your precious time on something that does not support your purpose here? Remember the people you are saying no to most likely want you to be happy, so you saying yes to something you would rather not do is not the intention behind asking you in the first place. We are adults, so we respond to life, not react to it; So have faith others will be okay with you saying no. By using a new system, letting go of items and saying no to others more often, the things we have control over, we can live the life intended for us; a simplified, organized and stress free life. This new way of life is a self-disciplined one but it is the only way we can create space and time for new adventures that are aligned with our life values to enter our lives. We have the power to say no, create a schedule and to bring items into our homes. Let's make the most efficient choices for ourselves and our families.

Chapter 6

I Am Worthy Of Having It All And Living In Abundance!

by Eva Macias

It's not your salary that makes you rich. It's your spending habits.
~ Charles A. Jaffe

Eva Macias

Eva Macias is the president of Eva Macias & Associates Financial & Insurance Services, a marketing firm representing many of the largest and most respected financial services companies in the world. Ms. Macias is also the founder of La Latina y Su Dinero, a financial literacy workshop that educates and empowers women to deal with their finances. She has recently consolidated her doctrine into a book and is now the author of A Woman's Guide to Money.

Ms. Macias has always been devoted to giving back to the community. She is a member for Amigas for my Soul, a non-profit organization that reaches out to the women of today to help empower and provide them with tools to build a better tomorrow. Ms. Macias is a powerful sought-after speaker in the financial world, speaking to students at California State University, Los Angeles, La Federacion Jaliciense, City of Los Angeles 9th District, and multiple Unified Schools Districts including Los Angeles Unified School District, about preplanning to maximize their retirement options.

fb: Eva Macias and Associates Financial and Insurance Services
ig: evamacias | Yelp: Eva Macias and Associates | LinkedIn: Eva Macias
www.evamacias.com | www.lalatinaysudinero.com

HAVE YOU EVER asked yourself how can I live abundantly if I live paycheck to paycheck? There are so many things we can do to live an abundant life, yet at times giving up our latte or coffee is not negotiable. We at times forget the TRUE power we hold. At times, it seems so impossible to give up the thing that is convenient like shopping, because from the push of a button, you can have anything delivered in 24hrs. This is why we are eating fast food because it is quick, easy and cheap.

The same things that give us so much pleasure, are the exact things that may cause STRESS in our lives.

What if there was a way to having it all?

Hello, my name is Eva Macias and I am a powerful, caring, compassionate financial expert. I grew up in what I call the "hood"; lack of resources and all I saw was violence in my city. Born and raised in L.A., I remember listening to gun shots more often than I wanted to. Both my parents did not attend college. They were hardworking people, but they lacked the education. Both my parents are self-taught. They taught themselves how to read and write. Being the youngest of 8 siblings, I always had someone "watching out" for me or telling me what to do. As I got older, I realized I lived in poverty, but as a kid I never really knew any better. Living in such neighborhoods, statistically I should have "failed" or gotten pregnant by age 19 or so. In our household, the women did all the household chores and the men, well, they worked. Our 2-bedroom house with 12 people in it, was in my eyes, a slumber party; but later in my adult life, I realized we lived in poverty. My mother collected welfare (for those who don't know what that is, it is government assistance) by the time I was 2 years old. I don't ever remember my family discussing money or even future goals. I bring this up because I really never had a formal education on money, besides work hard to get money to pay bills. I attended California State University of Fullerton. However, I did not start in finance because I was more like a confused college student, not knowing the direction my future would take. I worked many jobs to pay housing and transportation. One job really helped me get to the next level in life. I learnt a new relationship about money when I was 19 going on 20. I thought having a big house and expensive cars was what was called "success." I wanted that too! I worked really hard and got my first house at 23 years old and my second at 24 years old. At the time, I was 24 years old, making a six-figure income. WOW! I was living the dream, until the 2008 stock market crash changed my life. I was on the verge of losing my houses to foreclosure and having my cars repossessed. Credit companies were harassing me and threatening to sue me, and they did. My life was so full of fear, doubt and chaos. At this point, all I wanted was peace of mind, sleep and reaffirmation that everything would get better.

Now, I can say after the storm of chaos and fear, I saw the rainbow, but it took commitment, faith, and action on my part for it to work! I took baby steps until I started running with it. Now, I can say I still own my home after 11 years of being a homeowner, I own my own business with a few employees, I was on the radio, I will be coming out on the cover of the *Women of Distinctions* magazine 2017, I am now in the process of completing my second book. I am the Treasurer of an amazing non-profit organization that empowers women to live a BOLD, UNAPOLOGETIC life. I speak at California State University of Los Angeles on topics like financial literacy workshops. I have been blessed to share my knowledge with those who create the time to want a better future for not only their household but their communities.

I Don't Know How To Budget, Is There Still Hope For Me?

What I have found out based on majority of us, is that we never really master the basics of budgeting. Besides, how much money are we really supposed to allocate to housing, transportation and so on? Yes! There is still hope for those who want to shift their money to start working for them. Remember, it's not the amount of money you make, but the amount of money you keep. Using this formula will allow you to have it all. Use your net income, meaning after taxes have been removed from your paycheck. Use 35% of your money for housing, 15% on transportation, 20% on other living expenses, 15% on debt and 15% on savings.

Here is how you should bundle your top 5 categories:
- Housing: mortgage/rent, repairs, taxes, utilities, insurance
- Transportation: car payments, gas, insurance, repairs, parking/ tolls, train or bus fees.
- Other Living expenses: eating out, vacations, entertainment, clothing, groceries
- Debt: Student loans, credit cards and personal loans
- Savings, emergency money, retirement fund and a college fund for your kids

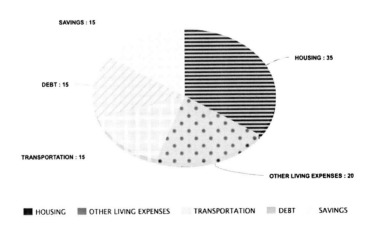

SAVINGS : 15 HOUSING : 35 DEBT : 15 TRANSPORTATION : 15 OTHER LIVING EXPENSES : 20

■ HOUSING ■ OTHER LIVING EXPENSES TRANSPORTATION DEBT SAVINGS

This will allow one to tell your money where it should go; not where it would like to go. The power of mastering the basic steps can ultimately create one's wealth.

I helped a family protect their money, but the interesting part was that the wife was a stay-at-home mom and the husband was the main provider. He had never made more than $50,000 of income in his life and yet had over $350,000.00 saved. Incredible! The week before, I had meet with an attorney who makes over $250,000.00 a year and had no savings besides about $20,000.00 in her checking account to pay for the upcoming bills. Again it's not the money, but what you do with the money.

It's so important we take control of our money or else our money takes control over us.

How Do I Save If I Don't Have Any Extra Money?

One of the biggest keys to having money is by managing the habit of spending. What I mean by that is this - Most people get a paycheck, pay bills, utilities and entertain themselves, then save. However, the best thing to do is to first SAVE about 15% of your paycheck and then pay bills and so forth. It's important to check the habit that one needs to break or stop in order to create abundance. The illustration below will help you see the difference when you save first then pay bills versus pay bills first and then save. See the following illustration:

Exhibt A		**Exhibit B**	
Paycheck	$5,000	Paycheck	$5,000
Rent/mtg	$2,500	Save 10%	$500
Utilities	$300	Rent/Mtg	$2,100
Car payment	$450	Utilities	$300
Car Insurance	$125	Car Payment	$350
Cell phone	$130	Car Insurance	$125
Grocories	$400	Cell Phone	$60
Fuel	$200	Groceries	$350
Entertainment	$400	Fuel	$200
Credit Cards	$300	Entertainment	$300
Savings	$100	Credit Cards	$200
Money Left Over	$95	Money left over	$415

How Do I Plan My Finances When I Don't Have Time Or Energy?

I often deal with many people who are very emotional about money. I always tell them that money has no emotion. There are some who are projecting their own feelings onto it. So, money is just money. We have the power to create time with money. Once we have an abundance of money, we allow ourselves to create time with the people we love and/or spend time doing what we love doing. Be consistent with the actions. Take time to cultivate great habits. Nobody ever has time until they **CREATE IT!** Most people do not take the time to look at their finances because of the fear of what might come up. The lack of time is usually lack of intimacy. We are afraid of looking within to see what's really going on. What I mean is…what fear is so present on your finances that it freezes us from creating a better future?

The lack of self -love and worthiness is the
core essence of not making time.

Maybe the fear is I am not good enough, I don't deserve it or the fear of the unknown. But when one starts looking at their finances with love and vision, some start seeing the power of how their money can work for them. When you take the time to see what areas of your finances need help, we can then apply ACTION behind them. It will only be a matter of time before one starts seeing RESULTS. For example, I had a young woman in her mid-30's, working 2 jobs, with about 32 credit cards, of which half were delinquent, and still living at home, telling me, "I don't have time." I ask her for 1 hour of her time. She brought 3 grocery bags full of bills, some open and unopened. After an hour of getting her organized, I was able to let her know there was hope for her. We met 2 other times that month for a total of about 3 hours. On the third visit, she committed to saving $700.00 a month. A year later, she has paid down 6 credit cards and she is now only working 1 job and is not stressed over finances because she knows she will have money as long as she continues with the plan. Notice how taking the time can shift the way we look at money. In just a matter of 1 year, a huge transformation has occurred. She never even thought it was possible. At the end of the day, taking the time to see this through can ultimately impact the future of one's families in so many different ways. At this point, money doesn't control your thoughts; Instead, you're in control. Choose to build the habit of deciding where your money should go.

In conclusion, age, sex, ethnicity or educational background should not dictate where you envision your financial security. It's important to take responsibility and be committed to take ACTION, in order for any vision to manifest. Helping one create peace of mind, abundant living, having it all and most importantly, sharing your experience and stories with those less fortunate than us. Wealth is a choice! What are the choices we can make to get closer to making wealth? Also, remember wealth for so many has a different meaning. LIVE in the power of your wealth, as only there can you learn to share with others the wealth of time, money and knowledge. I am always available to be at your service.

Chapter 7

Dear Stress, You Ain't Got Nothing On This Mother

by Sunit Suchdev

"Failing to plan is planning to fail. "
~ Alan Lakein

Sunit Suchdev

Sunit Suchdev is a skin care obsessed, health conscious fashionista who enjoys reality TV and shopping. She has spent the last 27 years of her life hustling, starting as a gymnastics coach at the age of 13, and collecting a paycheck in one form or another, her entire working life. Her primary interest has always been in coaching and training. She loves sharing her knowledge and helping people achieve their goals and dreams. It is hard for her to stay quiet when she knows someone could be happier! Sunit recently left a successful career in the corporate world to pursue her passion for inspiring women, particularly moms, to have it ALL. She has a positive "can do anything" attitude in life, and has never let any of the modern day stressors get in her way. Sunit does it ALL, with twin 4 year- old boys. Her new venture "Modern Mommy Prepschool" is an online course and podcast geared towards expecting mothers who know they want it all in motherhood, but don't quite know how. She eschews the mainstream ideas that foster negativity in moms these days. She believes you CAN have it all and encourages women to find their true purpose, put on some lipstick, and live their best life! Happy moms make happy babies and her goal is to empower and inspire women to grow businesses AND babies that will evolve to make this world a better place! Sunit lives in beautiful British Columbia with her ah-may-zing husband and super cool twins.

sunit@moderntwinmom.com
ig: @moderntwinmom | fb page: Modern Twin Mom

MANY PEOPLE THINK you can't plan motherhood, that it is something that happens TO you; That you should take your cues from your child and put everything else on hold. Perhaps, this is why it seems that so many mothers these days look like they are no longer able to focus on anything but their kids. In my experience, planning for motherhood helps to be prepared for what is to come. If you want to mom like a BOSS (yes I just turned the word "mom" into a verb), then approaching your family life the same way you approach your business will serve you well. If you are a woman on a mission to rock the business world (and since you are reading this book, I'm betting you are!), you certainly don't want babies to be holding you back. However, is it possible to have it all AND be a mom? I say, HELL YES. You can have ANYTHING YOU WANT, girlfriend! If you are a woman who is about to enter into mommyhood and you aren't sure if or how you can juggle both your business and your baby, I hope you will come away feeling inspired to have it all. And if you are a mom who didn't get a chance to plan ahead, but are willing to re-shift some priorities now, I think you will walk away with some great tips on what to start doing!

I have dealt with my fair share of stresses in life. How do I deal? Like a boss of course! You know what's really hard to do? Deal with stress like a boss when you have kids. There was a time when I didn't know if I could have kids. Everywhere I looked, women were having babies. It was gut wrenching. You know what was worse? When those women told me not to do it. Here I was, desperately wanting to have a child, and these women were telling me to stop trying so hard! In those days when I was in the depths of despair, feeling beaten down, one failed fertility treatment after another, I swore that would never be me. I had a life I loved and a career I was passionate about and I wasn't about to go through all this only to regret it. I wanted kids to ENHANCE my life, not take away from it. Luckily for me, I got to put my money where my mouth was. After many disappointments,

I got pregnant with not one, but TWO babies. I have encountered many challenges in life, but my biggest one lay ahead of me. I didn't want to give up anything in my life that I loved, but I now had TWO little humans to take care of. I was determined to do it all. I went on a mission to prove that it CAN be done. You CAN be an amazing mom, and have an amazing life that you love. Your kids can be a great addition to your team, instead of a detraction. I am not willing to sacrifice anything I am passionate about in life.

> As a mom of twins, I choose to deal with the stresses of life while keeping a smile on my face, because that is the face I choose to show my boys.

It IS possible to have it all and from this moment forward, I ask that you do one thing. **Stop listening to the people who say that you can't.** That striving for perfection and juggling both a career and babies means that you are sacrificing one or the other. It's not true. There is nothing wrong with aspiring to do it all, perfectly. Perfectionism is yours to define, and yours alone. You don't have to be perfect on anyone's terms other than your own. YOU get to choose how you deal with your business and your babies. **Do not, I repeat, do NOT, put your dreams on hold.** Saying, "I'll pick that back up when they are in school", or WORSE, "I'll follow my dreams when they don't need me anymore", does not serve you OR your kids! Be selfish. Be happy. Happy moms raise happy kids. And this world needs more of BOTH! You CAN be selfless when loving your kids, and be selfish when loving your SELF.

Know Thyself – Set The Intention For What You Want, And
Then Plan For It

By the time I got pregnant, I was successful and established in my
career, and had big dreams for myself. Everywhere I looked though,
women who had kids were completely crumbling. Husbands were
being put on back-burners. Careers were being dropped. Once I
finally got pregnant, I started hearing the comments. "You're going to
have your hands full!", "You probably won't want to work anymore!",
"Doesn't your job require a lot of travel? You won't be able to do that!"
I also know that there were people in my circle who didn't think I was
"the mothering type". Probably because I was so driven and did devote
so much to having a career and having it all.

They thought I was only capable of devoting
myself to one thing, but they didn't know me.

I go for gold. Whatever I want to do in life, I want to do it well. I most
certainly didn't want to give up the position I had worked to get to in
my career. I'm a juggler. A hustler. An eternal optimist. My biggest
asset? I'm a planner. I think ahead about what is important to me in
my life and I figure out how I'm going to make sure I can keep it. And
that is what I set out to do. I was having not one but TWO babies, and
I needed to figure out how to fit them into my already awesome life,
seamlessly.

I'll Have What She's Having - Pay Attention To Those Who
Are Doing What You Admire

So, I did what I do best. I started to google and research and read
books and blogs. I stopped listening to the nay-sayers who said it

couldn't be done and I started talking to the women who looked like they were rocking the mom thing. I never wanted to lose the things about my life that I loved and I was very clear about what those things were. Being able to indulge in some reality TV while enjoying a glass of wine, going on girls' trips, going back to work and always being able to work-whether it was a job outside the home or my own business. I wanted to be able to work out, eat healthy, and go to the bathroom without my kids sticking their fingers under the door (which is a thing I guess?). I wanted to continue eating at fine restaurants without needing a kid's menu. You know, just normal stuff! I talked to the moms who were doing all that and followed their advice. I then talked to my husband; my teammate and my partner. **You MUST communicate** with the second most important person in this "business" of babies. Your "business" partner! So many women make the mistake of wanting to take over with their mother's intuition and they don't allow the husband to help. Either they don't trust that he can do it as well as they can, or they don't want anyone interrupting their bonding time with the baby. Regardless of the reason, women are doing themselves a huge disservice when they decide to alienate the other parent. Before I had my boys, I had a lot of communication with my husband regarding what was important to us. Once we were on the same page, we agreed that we needed to put US first and this would be a team effort.

The Business Of Babies- A Business Plan And A Great Partnership Leads To Success

I knew I wanted to keep working and pursuing my passions. I wanted to raise awesome kids that would one day contribute positively to society, and I didn't want to sacrifice myself in the process. I set the intention, and I involved my partner. Together, we decided what kind of parents we wanted to be and then we talked to others who were parenting that way. We got on the same page, and we chatted about all that was important to us in family life, work life, and kids. I often refer to the "pillars" of motherhood, and your husband and your SELF are two of those pillars. Once we established what was important to us as a couple and where we wanted to be 2, 5, and even 10 years from now as people and as parents, we were able to work backwards and be more clear on our parenting approach. Do you know if you want to be an attachment parent? Helicopter parent? Free range? A tiger mom? Who knew there were so many categories? It's enough to make your head spin. Knowing your lifestyle, and your hopes and dreams for your family, will help you come up with a parenting plan. It's like a business plan, but with less dollar signs! One of my favorite sayings in parenting is, **"start as you mean to go"**. It's simple. If you don't want to be sleeping with your 4-year old every night while your husband gets relegated to the guest room, don't start that habit now. Be proactive. Don't wait for a "phase" to start and then try and figure out how to deal with it. You will be busy climbing the corporate ladder or running your own empire. Do you really want to have to be looking this stuff up as it happens? It's hard to go anywhere these days without being smacked in the face with a parenting website, blog, or book. Resources are literally at our fingertips! Take advantage!

Expect The Unexpected - And Bounce Back Like A Champ

So even after all that planning, guess what happened? Things didn't quite go as perfectly as I had planned. One of my twins ended up in the NICU and I ended up with Bell's palsy (google it, it's scary and it sucks). Add a c section recovery to that mix and you've got a whole lot of shitty days. But you know what? Being prepared also meant being prepared for the unknown. Things will not always go according to plan, but having a plan means you can navigate the tough waters and steer back on course when the time is right. Once we got out of the hospital, I continued with my "baby business plan" and I stuck to it. All the preparation has paid off. Yes, there were sleepless nights and many foggy days where I lived on coffee alone. But they were so few and far between, I don't really remember them. I also never talked about them. Sleepless nights and crying babies are a fact of parenting life. It should be no surprise to anyone and yet there is no shortage of new parents talking about it all the time. I've noticed a frightening trend these days. Moms complaining about, well, momming (there's that verb again). Mommy blogs that are profiting from candid discussions about the not so nice side of motherhood. The problem is, what you focus on, expands. If people aren't prepared for some tough days and trying nights once they become parents, they are living in a bubble. We all know what it's like, so why are we continually talking about something that is normal, as though it's a surprise? I would encourage all moms to focus on the amazing blessings that babies bring to our lives, instead of the short lived difficult early years. I promise you, if you have a plan and an intention to carry it through, without stopping to focus too much on the downsides, you will get through with flying colors, and both your baby and your business will thrive.

Happy Endings - Happy Moms Make Happy Families

Some may think that equating your babies to a business is ridiculous, but in reality, is it really that much of a stretch? You wouldn't start a business without a plan, so why would you approach motherhood that way? Both of these things are probably the riskiest and potentially most rewarding things you will EVER do. And they both require an immense investment. Not only did implementing a solid plan help me as a career woman, but it has elevated my relationship with my husband and given my kids some reliable expectations and boundaries within which we operate. I have had to sacrifice nothing to be both a great mom and a business woman. Spend 5 minutes with my kids and you'll know why I'm so proud of all the legwork I've put into parenting them. These days, I am working from home and the habits we have set up, allow me to do so while my kids are with me. It has truly been an awesome experience. I credit all our proactive planning and legwork.

Are you inspired? Hopefully you have gleaned a few ideas of what you can do as a business woman, entering motherhood or in the throes of it, to help you say goodbye to mommy stress.

It's always best to plan, but never too late to implement:

1. Set the intention. Your business or your career are important to you. If it's not something you want to give up, say it. Own it. Take care of your SELF first.

2. Surround yourself with positive, inspiring women who are moms AND career women. They do exist. Say no to the negativity and stop hanging out on forums where women have made it a pastime to complain about how their kids are sucking the life out of them.

3. Your partner in this venture is as important as any other business partner. Include them in everything.

4. Start as you mean to go. Have a plan. Start at the end and work backwards. Pay attention to other families. When you see someone doing what you're trying to do, ask them how they did it.

5. Don't get too comfortable. Life happens and things rarely ever go according to plan, but being prepared yet flexible, will help you stay focused and grounded when you veer off course!

Businesses and children that are the result of a purposeful plan are what this world needs more of. Say goodbye to the stress of juggling both. When you plan ahead, lead with your heart, and surround yourself with positivity, you can affect immense change in our world. Why do I care? Because my kids are going out into that world one day too. Let's make it a great place for all of us.

Come visit me at www.moderntwinmom.com to see what I'm up to and for some mommy inspiration!

Chapter 8

360☉° To Happiness

by Kathryn Yeatman

"Each morning we are born again. What we do today is what matters most."
~ Buddha

Kathryn Yeatman

Kathryn Yeatman, although born and raised in Canada, has lived in Los Angeles for 20 years. In 2001, she graduated Massage school and has been in the business ever since. Massage and bodywork has been Kathryn's passion since her early 20's. As a Certified Massage Therapist and a Certified Manual Lymphatic Drainage Therapist, Kathryn believes in a multi-dimensional approach to bodywork, and health in general, trusting that we are not simply what we can see or touch. This is why Kathryn has studied for hundreds of hours, learning many different and unique modalities to become the well-rounded therapist she is today. Some of her skills include: Massage Therapy (Circulatory/Swedish, Deep Tissue/Sports, Prenatal), Manual Lymphatic Drainage, Sensory Repatterning, Cranial Sacral Integrative Therapy, Acupressure as well as various modalities of Energy Healing. Kathryn is also an artist, musician, a lover of yoga & fitness and a previous restaurateur. As an artist, she has been creating and selling her original abstract art for many years. She is currently working on a series of original sacred geometry pieces. Kathryn's most recent passion is writing. She has begun writing a collection of children's books that focus on love, unity and kindness.

Being a mom however, is Kathryn's proudest accomplishment. Life changed forever after her daughter Sophia was born. She believes cultivating Sophia's happiness and guiding and nurturing her daughter through life is one of the keys to her success.

ig: @kat.cmt | fb: @katyeatmancmt
katcmt.com | kathryn-yeatman.pixels.com

WE'VE ALL HEARD the expression 'come full circle'. But what does it truly mean? Life has a funny way of revealing itself to us sometimes. The Universe gently guides us in the right direction towards a path of true content. If we waver from that path, sometimes we have to try again. Begin again. Or be put in front of the same path to make a different choice. The journey to self-fulfillment is no different. What makes you passionate? What makes you smile from ear to ear? What would you do today if you could do anything you dream of? The Universe, and our higher selves, wants us to be happy! There is no greater contribution to the vibration of the earth like a happy and fulfilled human being. When I was growing up, I would never have guessed where I would be today. I left Canada, followed my heart and got to a place where I just knew I was meant to be. But then, a few choices lead me down a road that led away from my heart. I've had to come full circle, back to me, to find my happiness again.

My 360° to happiness has been a long road towards the realization that to be happy, I must follow my innermost desires, to put myself first. I went from being an excited, confident and alive person, to one drowning in unhappiness. When I made the decision to put my passion and career on hold in order to pursue the dreams and desires of my husband, that's where it all started to go wrong. My husband had addictions to work, alcohol and most of all, stress. As the years passed, and the stress mounted, I began rationalizing why I wasn't feeling fulfilled. "I chose this life," I would say to myself. "I'm good at the job I agreed to do. I knew who he was when I said *I do*. "I can change him," I thought. But the one who was really changing was me. I was becoming a shell of myself. *The day I realized that I had chosen the wrong path for myself, was the day I woke up.* Where am I? Who have I become? And where am I going? After years of stress and struggle within myself, I decided to change my trajectory.

And so today, I have come full circle. I am single again, divorced, but I am in the career I was so excited about so long ago. I even have the same roommate as I did 18 years ago! It may seem as though 'I'm right back where I started', but the truth is that **I am different.** I have gained knowledge, experience, new perspective and a sense of self that I never would have realized without going through what I did. It turns out that after everything, and all those years, I am still passionate about the same things: family, love and career. Except now, I am happy and I no longer have an addiction to stress!

When I was 21, I left my home in Canada and moved to California, not knowing a soul. I was alone, free and daring. I managed to start a new life in Los Angeles and I stumbled upon my calling rather quickly. I was doing extra work in movies and TV and I would be on set for hours at a time, getting to know people and sitting around. I would instinctually begin massaging someone's shoulders, or hands, like it was second nature. People would tell me I was a natural, and why don't I go to massage school? At that point, I thought it sounded amazing, but how could I possibly afford it? Massage school was very expensive! Maybe someday, I thought.

Little did I know, that thought of mine shot out into the Universe, like a beam of light, and began to manifest. When an idea, dream or thought is from the purest source of you, it has no choice but to be fully realized. Sometimes we have no idea how or when it will happen. And sometimes, our negative thoughts and actions can block our own dreams before they come to fruition. We close the door before the door even appears. How many times have you thought, "Impossible. That will never happen." Or, "No way! I don't have the money for that." How about, "It's just a dream". These negative thoughts don't have any power unless you believe them. Self-limiting beliefs destroy the chance at manifesting our truest desires. Negative thoughts block our aspiring paths, lock the doors of destiny and darken our dreams. And what do we blame? We blame our situation, our circumstances, our parents, our childhood, and our partners.

By simply opening our hearts and minds to
what CAN BE, we are able to change our lives.
The possibilities are endless.

At 25, I still dreamed of going to massage school. It was still the lack of money that was stopping me. Then a funny thing happened. One day as I was leaving the apartment, I noticed the TV was still on. I went to turn it off and happened to catch the end of *Wheel of Fortune*. For some reason, I stopped to listen as the show mentioned it would be taping in Los Angeles and to send in a postcard if you wanted a chance to be a contestant. I grabbed a pen and scribbled down the address. I don't even remember the last time I had seen that show but hey! Why not?! I thought to myself, 'this is interesting'. It struck me as a sign; my intuition was speaking to me loud and clear. So I popped a small index card with my name and address on in it into the mail. Three months later, I received a letter saying that my card was randomly selected and was being offered an audition to be a contestant on the show! At that point, I just knew that this was meant to be. I began telling all my friends and family that I would be chosen and that I would win $50,000. Yes, I know, it sounds a little out there. Even my friends and family thought so. But I was so sure. I meditated on it every day. I began to feel what it would feel like to be on the show, to win and to have that money in my bank account. I planned how I would spend it: new used car, new bed, pay off debt, travel, and…massage school!

I made it through the auditions; I was one of 15 chosen out of hundreds. And I won the whole show, $56,000 in total. The night I won, I called my mom. I had been through this conversation many times during my meditations. "Hi mom. I did it!! I won!!" My friends and family were stunned. But I wasn't! That experience changed everything for me. I began to see that life is *limitless and we are limitless in manifesting our dreams.*

There I was, 27 years old and holding a check for $56,000. First thing I did was sign up for massage school. It proved to be everything I thought it would be. I had found something that I was very good at, and I really loved it. After massage school, while building my bodywork business, I worked as a server to make ends meet at an Italian restaurant. There I met Marco, a quirky and charming Italian man who owned the restaurant. He was 17 years older than me and not really my type. I never imagined I would end up dating and later marrying him. We all dream about finding love. I believed I had found the man of my dreams.

When Marco decided to open a new restaurant, he asked me to do it with him. This meant giving up my newfound career but I still said yes. After years of striving to become a massage therapist, I gave his life, his dreams more importance over my own. I believe that this was the pivotal point at which I chose the 'other' path. How could I have let my dreams go so easily? Why did I do it? I still don't really know the answer, but I know it changed me. So I put my massage table in the closet, and put 100% into my new career as a restaurateur.

Our new restaurant was wildly successful, set in the heart of Brentwood, California. We had celebrity clientele, write-ups in all the right publications and a wait list for a table. We appeared to make a pretty good team. We even decided to get married. It seemed like we were on top of the world! But behind the scenes was different. The stress that comes from owning a restaurant is extreme. We fought all the time while working together. I would end up locked in the bathroom crying and Marco would drink to relieve his stress. Marco had done this for many years and for him, stress was a life force of some sort, he despised it, yet craved it at the same time. I on the other hand, was not used to this! I was immersed in a never-ending stream of stress. We took it home with us, and it ruled our lives. But when we made money, Marco was in his own little heaven, and that's when he could make me feel good, feel like 'this is the man I married'. An off week at the restaurant meant a whole other ballgame. It was chaotic, extreme and draining and yet, I stayed.

After 5 years of managing the restaurant, I realized we couldn't work together anymore. I was drowning in sorrow. I suggested I start my massage career again and my husband laughed it off, telling me that I would never make money doing that. I think back on it now, at how that made me feel and I don't even remember. I was numb. Numb to my happiness, to my worth, to the value of my own dreams and desires. I had, after all, chosen this man and this path and I had to stick it out.

Our solution was to open a 2nd restaurant, because that's what stressaholics do! This will make us more money won't it? This will save our relationship, won't it? The answer was a resounding NO. We opened our new restaurant just in time for the big recession. And so it continued: the tides of happiness in our marriage followed the ups and downs of the businesses. He stayed at the first restaurant and I ran the new one. Instead of seeing each other at work all the time (and fighting), we saw each other at home, briefly in the mornings and I'd see the intoxicated personality of my husband at night. Sometimes on Monday, we would have a date night, but it wasn't guaranteed.

About a year after opening the second restaurant, my little sister had a baby. The experience made me realize that I also wanted a child. I asked my husband and he agreed to have one.

In 2010, we welcomed our beautiful baby girl, the love of my life, Sophia Simone. The first year of motherhood was an amazing, challenging and humbling experience. For me, having Sophia changed the way I looked at things. I started to feel more like myself and I started caring a little less about things that made me miserable before like fighting, problems at work, self-doubt, a distant relationship and the general stress of feeling unhappy. It was becoming clear to me. I was not myself anymore, or maybe I was just lost. I was bathing in a sea of stress that had swept me up and swallowed me whole. Sophia brought me back to myself, back to feeling love, joy, light, laughter and hope.

At the same time, business was getting worse. The recession had taken its toll, and this did not bode well for our marriage. Sophia was the one thing, I thought, that could change him. I thought maybe she had some magical fairy dust that will make him want to stop drinking, stop working so hard, stop creating stress in our lives, see me as an equal, and anything else I had an issue with. Well, I can tell you first hand, no one can change another human being if they don't want to change.

When my daughter was 2½, I asked for a divorce. It was the most devastating thing I've been through. I had to dig deep to find the courage, the strength to start a new life, to end an eleven-year relationship with the father of my child and to sell my business. I knew I could handle having Sophia on my own and as I opened myself up to a new beginning, things started to click. I could finally do what I've always wanted to do. But it wasn't easy. I had to go back to massage school, move to a small apartment, and navigate life as a newly single mom. Massage school the second time was very healing for me. All the bodywork I received, helped me to release all the stress and negativity that had accumulated in my body, mind and spirit. My energy was starting to flow again and my world was becoming my own again.

I am now working full time as a massage therapist and body worker. I have a whole new outlook on life. I am living life differently as well, with healthy habits and knowing that I have affected not only myself but also my child's life by *choosing* a new one. Even my relationship with my ex-husband is in a healthy, friendly state. I don't wake up feeling stress, anger, sadness or fear. Instead, I feel optimistic and happy. Of course, there are situations that arise which will bring momentary anxiety, but it's not a lingering, looming kind of stress. Ultimately, the answer was in me. All I had to do was find a way to listen, to circle back, and try again.

Here Are A Few Recommendations For Anyone Looking To Do A 360:

1. **Meditation** of any kind. I personally love the Deepak Chopra 21-day Guided Meditation challenges. They are free, guided and there is a new one every 3 months. Even closing your eyes in silence for 15 minutes a day can make incredible changes in your brain activity. Studies have shown that '… meditation helps relieve our subjective levels of anxiety and depression, and improve attention, concentration, and overall psychological well-being.' - Alice G. Walton, Forbes 2015. When we connect with the stillness through meditation, our awareness expands and we are united with our true selves.

2. **Self-reflection.** Giving yourself time at the end of each day to make a journal entry, say prayers or have thoughts of gratitude will center you and align yourself with your deepest desires. It also helps to let go of stress and anxiety through simply *getting it out.* Gratitude is one of the most important virtues to possess.

    'Gratitude is like a magnet; the more grateful you are, the more you will receive to be grateful for.' – Iyanla Vanzant

3. **Bodywork.** Stress manifests in the body in many ways: high blood pressure, headaches, muscle pain/tension, stomach upset, chest pain and much more. We are more than meets the eye. We have bones, tissues, body systems and energy fields, and it is important to receive bodywork that will affect positive change for our *whole selves.* There are many modalities proven to assist the body in relieving stress including Massage Therapy, Craniosacral Therapy, Acupuncture, Reiki, and many more. I urge people to try something new, research some

old and new types of healing bodywork and see what feels good! The benefits are endless, especially for stress reduction.

4. **Exercise** is another game changer. Not only is exercise healthy for your cardiovascular system and muscular system, it also boosts endorphin levels. In essence, it makes you feel good. Any form of exercise is a form of self-love. It takes discipline to begin a healthy exercise routine but the payoff is well worth it.

What do you need to change to make a 360 to find *your* happiness? Be kind to yourself. Live in the moment. Breathe. Choose the path of joy and soon, the answer will be revealed.

Section 3

✦⟩✕⟨✦

Healing The Body With Knowledge

featuring

Medical Momma Kyla Thomson, Dr. Lauren E. Karatanevski, Survivor and
Thriver AJ Roy, Kimberly Francis RN, and Amanda Yeatman CHC.

Editorial commentary by Ky-Lee Hanson

THERE COMES A time where you may have your schedule, dreams, finances and all other priorities in place and then life decides to throw you the biggest curve ball of them all. Illness in a loved one, in a child. We will not always be prepared for impact, some are unimaginable but we can do our best to have a stress free, systematic life so that when the worst happens, we can survive it. Not everything in life always makes sense. There's not always a practical or trackable reason but we always have one consistent choice, to give up or to come out stronger. When all else fails, we must persevere. Medical Momma Kyla Thomson will teach us this. She makes us think about family and love and brings us to evaluate if we are prepared for the unforeseeable. Something consistent throughout this book is the message of education. As individuals, we need to empower ourselves wherever and whenever we can.

We are now thinking - what is stress, really? We have heard various ways it can show up in our life and the roles it could play. Stress comes in different shapes and forms and is different to various people. We know stress can have effects on your relationships with people and yourself, how you perceive your life and your work. We can be consumed with day to day activities and wear ourselves thin. We know our mind is affected by stress but what effects does it have on the body? How does the body respond? Is stress *actually* a real thing that can come with physical symptoms? Maybe if we can recognize what stress looks like on us, we could communicate with our body. We may be able to feel the mental and physical strains of stress but what about at a cellular level? Could stress lead to abnormal cell behavior or even disease?

These next chapters will help us to understand stress, the good and the bad, including from a scientific standpoint. Medical Momma Kyla Thomson, Dr. Lauren E. Karatanevski, Kimberly Francis RN, Amanda Yeatman CHC and Survivor and Thriver AJ Roy, discuss how to combat and defeat stress to better ourselves by utilizing western, eastern and holistic practices - what I like to call - integrative medicine.

Can we control and prevent stress? Although some disease has no practical rhyme or reason, can we at least play a role in the outcome, prevention, aiding or reversal of some conditions and symptoms? Do foods play any role on stress levels, good or bad? Science now says yes. Our epigenome which consists of a record of the chemical changes to the DNA and histone proteins - any of a group of basic proteins found in chromatin - of an organism; these changes can be inherited or occur from environmental influences, such as a person's diet, habits and exposure to pollutants. The chemical compounds of the epigenome are not part of the DNA sequence but are on or attached to the DNA and is involved in regulating gene expression "activity", development, tissue differentiation, and suppression of transposable elements. It is interesting to know that generations of gene code can actually be influenced positively or negatively by stressors – external and internal.

Laurie,
Thank you so much
for the love &
support for Bella.
Kyla Th

Chapter 9

Surviving Stress

by Kyla Thomson

"Some of us are never out of the woods, we live here… where life throws lemons at us while we gaze towards the light at the end of the tunnel. So, we crank our music, grab the tequila and party in the dark." ~ Kyla Thomson

Kyla Thomson

Before Kyla became the mom of a medically complex child, she received her Bachelor of Education at the University of Regina, became a Special Ed teacher and settled back into her home town of Swift Current, Saskatchewan where her and her husband dreamt of starting their family. Family at home was put on hold with their first child. The multiple rare conditions and life threatening scenarios her baby girl endured began at just three days old and progressed to living 58⊙ days in hospital, all from a province away from home.

From this battle, Kyla found a strength that would mold her purpose: supporting medical parents and all those impacting their lives including nurses, doctors, family, counsellors and more. After year one in the hospital, Kyla began a blog, YouTube Channel and Facebook Progress Page. These platforms provide Kyla with the outlet to mentor and coach, share her public speaking/media experiences, and raise awareness for all the charities and organizations involved in her daughter's life.

Kyla Thomson is a woman who has fought through the agony of miscarriage, put her career on hold, and withstood two years in hospital as a first time mom. She is the kind of person who will pour her heart out and lay it all out on the line just to help others. Her chapter can help you not just break up with stress, but assassinate it from some of the worst situations life throws at you.

fb: Isabella's Mustard Seed | youtube: Hospital Mom Hacks
blog: bellasmustardseed.blogspot.ca

I WOULD NOT wish the life my daughter and I have lived in hospital, on my worst enemy. I've been shaken to the core by the countless procedures on her tiny body, the hundreds of needle pokes she endured, twelve surgeries and the close calls with death. I lived in a hospital. I woke up to code blues and monitors beeping, shaking me from one terrified state to another. Oh I'm not just breaking up with stress, I've paid a hitman.

Our Story

At three days old, my daughter, Isabella, had her first of twelve surgeries. It left the first of many scars on her tiny body and my heart. My baby girl's first diagnosis was a bowel disease called Hirschsprungs. This evil disease meant the dead parts of her colon formed a blockage and lead to 5 bowel surgeries, months where she couldn't be fed, and an aversion to eating and drinking. Every other week we thought the fix would come and we could go home. It didn't come. My baby girl was always critically sick, not getting better and we couldn't figure out why. She was also born with a deadly disease no one knew she had, SCID (Severe Combined Immunodeficiency). She was born with no immune system and we did not know it. It was a miracle she survived until she was diagnosed at 11 months old, it was a miracle she lived at all. 11 months spent in hospital and her only cure meant preparing to live in hospital 11 more. I remember breaking into tears when they sat my husband and I down and told us we still could not take our baby girl home... I was broken. Her cure was chemotherapy followed by a bone marrow transplant, which would give her a new immune system. It was bittersweet to finally have a reason why she was never getting better, a curable diagnosis, but it also meant our life in hospital was about to get longer.

Manage & Conquer Stress

My daughter's start to life has been so extremely rare, it's hard to imagine how I survived such debilitating stress for so long. But I did. Three things stood at the core of how I conquered stress through probably one of the most unique ways a child and mother could begin their lives together: Surrounding myself with what made me happy, writing, and always remembering I do not have to live with stress. Through this I realized a combination of two things that allowed me to manage the stress in my life: Identifying what others could do for me and finding out what I could do for myself.

Surround Yourself With What Makes You Happy. No literally... Do this.

Music, comedy, memes, positive quotes: these were never out of reach and always within sight. I lived 10 months in isolation in a hospital room. It's quite painful to recount all the horrific things I had seen my daughter and many other children go through from the hospitals we lived in. The isolation I am talking about is the kind where no one was allowed to enter my daughter's hospital room without gowns, gloves, masks and booties. Before and during her bone marrow transplant, a bubble needed to be created for her and I to live in, to limit the risk for infections. It caused stress that suffocated me. I felt locked in a box. Keeping the strength to find ways to help my daughter develop in that room, became harder and harder.

I needed to turn that isolation room from a lonely jail cell into a positive oasis.

I needed to chase that fear from my mind every possible waking second; like when you watch a horror movie at night and need to turn on all the lights afterwards and watch a comedy just so you can fall asleep not believing in ghosts.

I posted concrete visuals all over the walls, on my phone screen, iPad screen, the whiteboard in the room and even used window markers. Any second I needed to draw my mind from spiraling negatively, I had that joke to make me laugh, or inspiring quote to remind me it WILL be ok. It helped lighten the mood in the room too. I found a lot of my daughter's nurses enjoyed my comedy. They saw how it helped me, made them more personable with me and took the stress out of the room when those stiff doctors came for rounds. I also began to crave music. I found it more and more healing and soon I realized that in those moments of calmness after the storm that sometimes that stress wasn't even real. Music was number one. I kept my Bluetooth speaker on my favorite stations and always had my headphones for the moments I left my daughter's room. Songs can draw out emotion to help you address and deal with your stresses and they can also help you heal while the stress dissipates. I have found that silence can make your mind race, spiraling into worsening thoughts, negative thoughts that choke your hope and happiness. Scrap that shit. Put some music on. Use it as a tool and bust up those stress demons. My Stress Busting Songs (You'll love these): Hailstorm – Here's To Us, Shinedown – Unity, Foo Fighters – Walk, & Outfield- Your Love (Play the air drums to this one, you know you want to.)

For me, music and comedy are the things that have always made me happy. For you, it might be a certain color, nature, or sports. Identify what that is, and incorporate elements of it into your daily life.

Write It ALL Down!

Stress eats your memory; devours it. It can also paralyze your speech. I found this happening to me every time I tried to speak to a family member about how I felt or inform my daughter's new nurse about her past surgeries. Sometimes when the stress became so great, I could not physically put my thoughts and questions into actual words and sentences. The fears and confusion in my mind could not get out of the way to make a coherent thought, until I started writing.

I wrote for myself to organize my thoughts and, in turn, it enabled my daughter's care providers to help more effectively. The confusion involved in my daughter's first year in hospital was astronomical. She was a genetic mystery, always sick and for 11 months, no one realized why she was always sick and never getting better, even at the hand of accomplished surgeons and specialists. Her deadly condition was not yet diagnosed. Daily, I was her only constant. Every nurse's shift change, every resident and doctor's rotation, and every new specialist that they thought she needed, brought daily discussions to my face. I was constantly on the hot seat, required to give every new medical professional an update of what worked that week and what didn't. Did she vomit a little, a handful or 300mls? What color was it? What texture? How labored was her breathing? When was the last NG change, ostomy change, dressing change? I started writing. Noting on everything I could: the napkin, my phone, a notebook. This turned into a record binder I developed with templates that only required a simple tick under certain boxes. I found the conversations with doctors became easier and easier. I got to the point where the stress of speech was no longer a jumbled ball in my mind, but instead, organized, coherent thoughts on paper that I could simply hand over to the doctor vs fumbling through my words. After a sleepless night, my record binder or note-page laying at my daughter's bedside could provide her new nurse with quick and valuable information when I was just too exhausted to speak.

Writing is healing. I could take the pain and turn it into purpose, so I began my blog. This journaling changed my medical mom hospital life world. The more I wrote, the more everyone understood. It led to so many people understanding and having the confidence to help me kill the stress in my life. Family, friends and the parent I just met down the Unit hall, began to understand what helps and what hinders. I soon found that when I explained the turmoil in my life through writing, I was in turn, helping others as well. I began receiving more and more acknowledgments for my blog posts, which pushed me to start sharing my writing in more ways.

Sharing what I wrote was a virtual tunnel from my daughter's hospital room, to the people I encountered outside the hospital. I constantly had everyone around me asking me questions. "How are you? How's your day? How's Bella?" Simple questions right? Wrong! I was drained from this life of living in hospital in isolation. How am I? Stab me in the eye with a pencil, about sums up how I am. I realized actually telling people that left them in shock as they just stood there with their mouths open and I continued on my way. Some probably thought I was nuts, but I was being honest. The truth is, that very simple question became an evil daily stress and it began making me angry and more stressed. Seeing other children playing with friends, eating, having fun at a park, going home with their families… I did not get those luxuries with my baby girl. Knowing someone is going to ask me this again, tortured me. But it pushed me to create a preventative solution and relieve myself of this stress. On day 572 in hospital, I updated my blog with this note:

'With my most exhausted, yet kindest intent: Don't ask me how I am doing, that forces me to respond. Any medical parent is saving every ounce of their energy to respond to their child, not your questions. Don't ask me what you can do, Again, that forces me to respond. No energy left for you and your questions. Just know what I need and do it, or make your best guess.' ~ Medical Momma

This changed my world. I had other medical moms around me

thank me for giving them what they needed to say but just didn't know how. Some may find it a tad harsh, but what worked was the fact that its boldness in a written format allowed those who really cared, to truly understand my pain and help me through.

Apart from my walls decorated with visuals of what made my daughter and I smile, they were also plastered with sticky notes. My daughter's medications changed more often than the weather in Saskatchewan. I could barely remember the long name of the med let alone the affects it had on my daughter's mind and body. Steroids were a bad one. My little girl, barely two years old and roid raging. I would scramble, trying to understand how what I did just yesterday was no longer comforting or calming her, but instead sent her into what I can only best describe as an agonizing Hulk-like rage. I would break into tears not knowing why she was hurting or why her mood would change so rapidly...the medication. I needed the bright sticky notes flashing at me as if they were a neon electrical signs saying, "Relax, remember this medication can cause this for this amount of time." I could make a note and remember what helped calm her when her own body was working against her. I would read these notes before bed, memorize them, embed them in my brain, so that that evil confusion causing stress monster would soon show up less and less.

I wrote to help myself gather my thoughts, educate those around me, and provide support for other people in a similar situation. Writing to kill the stress doesn't need to be in a public setting. The sticky notes provided reassurance for just me. Whether you choose a notebook, a blog, or the palm of your hand, write down your thoughts to organize them. Everything will become simpler.

You Do NOT Have To Live With The Stress ... Write That Down.

I am living proof that a person could be living with an obvious stress in their lives, and no mental health support is offered to conquer and manage that stress. I was a first time mom living in a Children's hospital... I knew the crazy rare hospital life I was living was not normal. Sure, people spent weeks and months in hospitals before... but years?! I wasn't sleeping, ever...did I need meds? Did the septic shock episodes that nearly killed my daughter twice, cause me to have PTSD? Do I use that term on myself? What is it actually doing to my mind, my life? For over a year, I did not know I didn't have to live with the horrible toll it all took on my mind, body and soul. It took me over a year to seek out Mental Health and I am so thankful I did. Three different hospitals and four different Social Workers did not offer me any form of Mental Health Support, I had to seek it out on my own. Yes, it is highly likely I could have benefited significantly from Mental Health support during the time I lived in hospital, but I never actually knew what I was looking for or what it was even called. It was never offered and so I never knew I needed it, but looking back...my God it could have saved me so much pain.

When the time finally came to transition from hospital life to home life, I was so unprepared and terrified. I began to have flashbacks of horrible memories stop me in my tracks while walking in my hallway or kitchen and force me to gasp for air as I choked on re-living that memory. I was petrified to even go out to the store and get groceries.

The triggers that set off bouts of spiraling stress in my mind, I didn't even know were called triggers.

I was finally home with my daughter and I slept less and less, waking up numerous times in the night because I couldn't rest until I physically saw her chest rise and fall with every breath as she slept. Constantly re-living every agonizing negative scenario we lived through could not be my only option.

I knew I needed help, and so I made it happen for myself. I found a family doctor and explained all of which I just explained to you. After hearing the summary of my daughter's story, he paused for a moment in shock, then immediately got me in touch with a Registered Psychiatric Nurse and Psychologist and thus my mental health support began. I refused to believe I had no other options other than living with this harsh stress, day after day. When no one offered me options, I made a point of seeking one out and making my life stress free. I knew then, I had survived and did not have to live with stress... the healing began.

Currently, my husband, daughter and I are doing well at home. Isabella is my warrior, she is my daughter, my everything. Though she still has a tough road ahead, we are even stronger now than at the start. We continue to battle a world unfamiliar with immune suppression, but the tools we have acquired equip us for victory. I can be the fierce momma bear who has the strength to lift her daughter up and through any obstacle that comes her way with my knowledge of overcoming stress and mental health support. We invite you to join us on our Facebook progress page, *Isabella's Mustard Seed*, to see how we continue to survive and conquer.

Chapter 10

Got Stress? - A Holistic View On Stress Management

by Dr. Lauren E. Karatanevski

"Being in control of your life and having realistic expectations about your day-to-day challenges are the keys to stress management, which is perhaps the most important ingredient to living a happy, healthy and rewarding life. "
~ Marilu Henner

Dr. Lauren E. Karatanevski

Dr. Lauren is an evidence-based Chiropractor and the co-owner of the Back in Action Health Clinic and the Oakville OptiHealth Clinic. Dr. Lauren believes in treating her patients the way she would want to be treated. She offers a holistic approach to care and has committed herself to creating an environment that allows her patients deal with pain, optimize health, prevent injury, and work toward achieving a pain-free fully functioning lifestyle.

Early in her career, Dr. Lauren saw the physical manifestations of stress in her patients and as such, developed a stress management program to help educate her patients to recognize how stress can affect one's body, one's thoughts, feelings and behaviors. She utilizes her program to help her patients get a jump on strategizing and managing their stress and symptoms.

Dr. Lauren is passionate in mentoring individuals in achieving their goals and dreams. She utilizes her own experiences as well as her research in the field of self-help, to assist individuals work toward attracting the life they want. Prior to her career as a Chiropractor, Dr. Lauren studied Kinesiology at the University of North Carolina Chapel Hill and competed as an international level springboard diver. She is also an International Best Selling Author for her work in Manifesting a New Life: Your Magical Guide to Attracting the Life that you Want.

www.drlaurenk.com | www.backinaction.ca
fb: facebook.com/drlaurenbia | t: @drlaurenbia | ig: drlaurenbia
LinkedIn: ca.linkedin.com/in/lauren-elise-Karatanevski-20b08255

Dear Diary,

I read in a magazine that expressive writing is a great tool for processing negative thoughts and feelings. Essentially, writing your way to a better frame of mind. So, here I am... writing to you because this way I can unload without judgement, criticism and the risk of crying or screaming. A friend of mine told me today, "It's not the load that weighs you down. It's how you carry it". I can tell you - I feel like Atlas with the world on his shoulders except I'm not as strong as he is. I feel the stiffness in my neck, the headaches, and the sharp pain in my back, the shortness of breath and the ability to burst out in tears when someone asks, "How are you doing?" The world is so heavy I don't have the stamina, strength or endurance to hold it up - it's going to crush me. Some days seem more balanced than others, but lately I feel like I've reached the tipping point on the scale. I've lost myself and I'm not happy. This feeling has been mounting for a while but it was last week where the timer on my ability to keep my cool was counting down to zero. 3, 2, 1 -- BOOM! I exploded. I had just come home from my morning workout and could hear the washer in the middle of its spin cycle. When the timer to the washer went off, I noticed that Michael didn't separate our clothes by colors and my white workout top was dyed a salmon pink. Ordinarily, I wouldn't care but this time around was different. I had just come home from a stressful trip to a dying front lawn, an empty fridge, a dirty house and a bunch of paperwork from the office that wasn't going to write itself. After my raging Hulk moment, I thought maybe I've done this to myself. I didn't think I would have to mention that working a 10-hour day, dealing with our other businesses, attending business meetings, planning a wedding, making dinner, going grocery shopping, doing the laundry, folding clothes, keeping the house clean, feeding and walking the dog etc...is a little too much for me to handle and I feel like a one-woman circus. I was overwhelmed. I was in desperate need for help - how could he not see it? Well maybe he did see it, which is why he did the laundry... but still. That day in a really loud voice and with a lot of tears I explained to him that I couldn't handle the stress and I'm burnt out - good news - it resonated with the both of us. In the period of calmness after my meltdown, I realized that I will never be the best version of myself if I think I can do everything on my own. On top of that, I need to re-teach myself to stop and smell the roses and find the joy in everything I am doing. I started sifting through quotes before I started writing to you and came across this, "Don't be shy about asking for help. It doesn't mean you're weak, it only means you're wise." I'll definitely remember that for the future.

Thanks for listening,
Lauren

What Is Stress?

Over 80 years ago, Austrian-Canadian endocrinologist Hans Seyle defined stress as, "The non-specific response of the body to any demand for change", or more simply put, "The rate of wear and tear on the body". In his research, Seyle discovered that in moments of happiness or despair, the body still undergoes stress; however, the effects on the body are different. He defined stress in two ways: Eustress or "good stress", and distress or "bad stress", and realized that our physical and mental state is altered based on how well we adapt to these stresses. To prove the effects of stress, Seyle experimented on animals by using noxious stimuli and observed the outcomes. He noted that noxious stimuli or "bad stress" such as deafening noises, blinding light, extreme climate changes and ongoing irritation all caused the animals to exhibit physical changes like ulcers and enlarged adrenal glands. He also hypothesized that persistent "bad stress" could cause the animals to develop chronic disease such as heart attack, stroke, and inflammatory arthritis.

As we have evolved, stress has become more of a popular subjective buzzword rather than a definition based on scientific findings. We have created the word stress to have several definitions as it means different things to different people. Some people use stress to define the towering amount of paperwork at the office while dealing with an unsupportive and critical boss. To others, it can be referred to as taking care of your children while working full time. For some, stress may be the moment where you have to cope with a sick parent or child. It can also be defined as a physical manifestation in the form of chest pain, neck pain, headaches, heart burn, stomach problems and loss of sleep. While we have diverted away from a scientific definition of stress, we can agree that the inability to adapt to good or bad situations is always stressful and will cause wear and tear on the body.

The Human Function Curve

An excellent way to describe how we adjust to stress in good or bad ways can be illustrated in *The Human Function Curve*, adapted from Nixon, P: Practitioner, 1979[1] (see the figure below). The curve is unique in that it represents an individual's level of functioning based on the relationship between stress (good and bad) and performance (physical and mental). Keep in mind, each individual will have a different curve based on what they perceive as stressful, however the outcomes are the same: exhaustion, ill health and breakdown are the result of an overly stressed-out person.

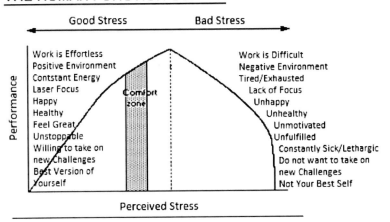

Eustress

Eustress is considered "good stress". It is a healthy amount of stress in your day-to-day activity that does not impact your mind or body and leaves you with a positive feeling or experience. Eustress can be the euphoric feeling following exercise or it can be the feeling you have after you have accomplished a goal or helped a friend in need. It improves performance and leaves you motivated, fulfilled, and happy.

The Comfort Zone

The Comfort Zone is a part of Eustress where your healthy stress encourages optimal performance and functioning. Your perceived stress and anxiety is in a balanced and neutral state. You are in control of your thoughts, actions, stressors, mind and body. Work feels effortless and your work environment is positive. You have a constant source of energy and you have laser focus. You feel and can accomplish anything you set your mind to.

A Side Note: The Comfort Zone as a part of the Human Function Curve is very different than the term "comfort zone" commonly used by life and business coaches. To these coaches, "comfort zone" means a negative period of self-growth that prevents you from reaching your true potential. These coaches require that you break away from this comfort and challenge yourself with new thoughts, ideas and actions. The idea is that you need to "get comfortable with being uncomfortable" when you want to grow as an individual. They believe that challenging yourself will create different adaptations and stressors that will result in positive self-growth outcomes.

Both these definitions of comfort zone can be used to create a zone of optimal performance. It requires "healthy stress", self-growth, new thoughts, new ideas, the ability to challenge yourself and openness to adapt to these challenges that will create the absolute best version of yourself. When you have reached this point, your perceived stress and anxiety will neutralize and you will take control over your mind and body.

Distress

Distress is considered "bad stress". It is an unhealthy amount of stress in your day-to-day activity that impacts your mind and body. You are unable to cope and manage with this stress. It is the stress that is exhausting, decreases your performance and leaves you unhappy, unmotivated and unfulfilled.

At this point, you may experience subtle signs of your stress mounting such as increased heart rate, rapid breathing, sweating, emptiness in your stomach, the onset of digestive issues, lack of sleep, tension in the shoulders, and tension in the neck and headaches. One will often ignore these signs and chalk them up as normal day-to-day reactions, however, the problem arises in that if they are ignored for too long, your body will undergo a state of exhaustion and start to break down until you burn out, you become ill, or you lose your ability to perform and function optimally.

Look for these physical and mental signs/symptoms that are common in a state of distress.

Physical symptoms of stress may include:
- Sensitivity to light and sound
- Frequent Colds
- Recurrent infections
- Inflammation in joints and muscles
- Decreased ability to heal
- Heartburn
- Reflux problems
- Stomach pains
- Digestive problems

Mental symptoms of stress may include:
- Anxiety
- Insomnia
- Fear
- Irritability
- Anger

- Unexplained Despair
- Unexplained Sadness

A constant unhealthy amount of stress for a period of time beyond three months is considered chronic. The mind and body become less resilient to change and your body's immunity to fight against its stressors decreases. The result is breakdown and illness. Some common physical manifestations of chronic stress include: decreased cellular function and increased free radical damage, the increase risk of cardiovascular disease and stroke, brittle bones and weak atrophied muscles, the increased risk of neurodegenerative disease and cancer.

Stress can be perceived as good or bad, healthy or unhealthy. It is not meant to be overwhelming or excessive, however living in a constant state of stress day in and day out, takes a toll on your physical and mental health.

A part of successful stress management is
your ability to recognize whether or not you
are moving out of a state of eustress
into a state of distress.

This requires that you are mindful of the signs/symptoms that are a result from stress and then implement effective strategies to move your stress back to a state where you can function optimally.

Stress Management

The towering amounts of paperwork. The unsupportive boss. The non-stop bills. The responsibility to your family. The tight shoulders, headaches and neck pain. The never ending list of to-do's without enough hours in the day to complete them. You may feel that there is no way to manage all the stress in your life, but you have more control than you think.

Stress management is about taking charge of your perceptions, emotions and the way you deal with the problems causing your stress.

Here are a few helpful tips to managing your stress:
1. Recognize your Stressors
2. Get Up and Move! / It's all about Micro-Breaks!
3. Watch what you Eat and Boost your Antioxidants

Recognize Your Stressors

Life today is full of being on the go, biting off more than you can chew, frustrations, deadlines, and demands. Stress has become so integrated in your life, that you likely do not notice it anymore. A part of successful stress management is your ability to recognize what is bogging you down.

By recognizing the symptoms and causes of your stress, you can take the first step to reducing its harmful effects and improve your quality of life. One question to ask yourself - Do you create your own stress? Identify your triggers and write them in a journal. A journal is a great outlet for you to get all your thoughts and feelings voiced without internalizing them or deflecting them onto others.

Tips on Identifying your Stress:

1. Outline the situation that has increased your levels of stress
2. Discuss the circumstance, the location and the people related to this situation
3. Identify what triggered the stress in the first place
4. Identify how you felt related to that stressor
5. Write down why you reacted the way you did toward that

stressor
6. Write down how you will manage the stress

By recognizing your triggers, it is easier to lessen the burden that you often times create for yourself. You can build a resiliency to your stress when you learn from those triggers and you increase your ability to persevere through challenges.

Get Up And Move! It's All About Micro-Breaks!

Research shows that we spend 75% of our day sitting. This sedentary behavior contributes to the stress you may feel when dealing with deadlines, customers and colleagues. Physical activity is integral in reducing and preventing the effects of stress. Any form of activity can help relieve stress and melt away tension, anger and frustration. Being active releases endorphins or your "happy hormones" which help boost your mood and make you feel good. To avoid getting caught in the despair of work related stress, start taking micro-breaks to break up your day.

Tips for Micro-Breaking:

1. Set a timer on your phone to remind you to get up and move.
2. The timer should be set every 30-40 minutes and you should do at least 1.5 minutes of activity. This could be anything from walking around the office, doing squats at your desk or doing some neck and shoulder range of motion exercises. This will help activate your muscles, get your blood flowing and release your endorphins.
3. Remember, your work is not going anywhere - remind yourself that 1.5 minutes of activity every 40 minutes will render you more productive, happier and less stressed while working.

4. Buy a Pedometer/Fitness Tracker: Pedometer technology is amazing when it comes to getting you active. There are many brands including the FitBit, Jawbone, MisFit, Garmin, Polar etc. each with their own tracking system to how you move throughout the day. You have the ability to set the number of steps you would like to achieve and it will remind you to move if you have been sedentary for too long.

Watch What You Eat And Boost Your Antioxidants

There is an unbelievable power in nutrition and stress can bring out the worse in our eating habits. It is not likely that in a stressful situation you would eat carrots and celery to minimize your stress levels. Rather, you bring out the chips, the candy, the alcohol and the ice cream. Your diet can have a profound effect on your stress and sense of well-being.

Tips for eating better in period of stress:

What to eat more of:
- Fruits and Vegetables/Legumes
- High Quality Protein: grass fed meat, organic chicken, wild fish
- Good Fats
- Nuts and Seeds

What to stay away from:
- Processed foods
- Refined Sugars
- Refined Carbohydrates
- Dairy
- Alcohol and Caffeine

New research is showing that we can encourage the body to protect itself by igniting its own internal antioxidant defense system. The idea of making antioxidants compared to the standard approach of taking antioxidants is a fundamentally-different approach to protecting the body from stress. About 20 years ago, a protein called NRF2 was discovered to regulate the body's ability to produce its own antioxidants such as catalase, superoxide dismutase and glutathione. NRF2 can be activated through proper exercise, nutrition and specific supplementation. Think of NRF2 as a thermostat within our cells that senses the level of stress in our body. When our body senses an accumulation of stress from the internal or external environment, NRF2 turns on our cells to make their own medicine to help us survive and thrive in stressful situations.

Stress can be considered good or bad but the outcome is still the same - wear and tear on the body.

> The good news - you have the ability to create or control your stress.

By recognizing the symptoms and causes of your stress, you can take the first steps to reducing its harmful effects and improve your quality of life. With strategies like recognizing your stressors, being active and eating well, you can build a resiliency to your stress at the same time, increase your ability to preserve through challenges. You can take control and find your "comfort zone" and excel at anything you set your mind to. Break up with your stress and be fabulous – You can do it!

[1] Nixon PG., The Human Function Curve – A paradigm for our times. Act Nerv Super (Praha). 1982; Suppl 3 (Pt 1):130-3.

Chapter 11

PERCEPTION

AJ Roy

———◆✖◆———

My life quote: There is no reason to look back, when there is so much good in front of you.

AJ Roy

AJ Roy was raised in the country. She now lives in the city, but is a country girl at heart. She obtained a diploma in Social Work at Algonquin College in 1987, hoping to make a career out of helping people. The lack of jobs in the domain prompted her to look elsewhere. She then decided to make a career working for the Federal Government to which she now has 25 years of service under her belt. Since 2000, she has been working at Transport Canada. She is presently a Safety Analyst working in Aviation.

Although she loves her socially-achieved career with the government, and her teammates, she has always had that burning desire to follow social work and help herself and others. Throughout the years, she has secretly been battling depression and anxiety, which continued to haunt her. The day she reached rock bottom, she decided to look depression and anxiety straight in the eye and shouting out loud, she said, "I'm breaking up with you!".

Through perseverance, courage, resilience and her love of life, she made it through. You can read her triumph in this book. This is her way of paying forward and getting back to her dream of helping people. An Occupational Therapist once told her "You are like a train; there's been stops along the way, some stops longer than others, but you keep going." People say that she lights up a room with her smile. Even on darker days, she still smiles.

aj.roy@mail.com | fb: www.facebook.com/arielle.roy.963

PERCEPTION

I Can Breathe Again…
by: AJ Roy

The days are long, and the nights are endless. It's been rainy, windy and cold for a very long time. I don't remember the last time I've seen the sun. I'm not even sure what it looks like anymore. When is my sentence going to end? –

There is despair and agony in every second of every day. Even through the numbness, I can still feel the pain. Deliver me from this dark and sinister hell. –

The road to salvation is nowhere near. I'm lost in the fog, and I can't seem to find inner peace. In the darkness, I'm alive, but so alone. The world has no colors. It's all black and white. I forgot my dreams, and left my love a long time ago. The pain is unbearable. –

I'm so cold that I can see my breath in the darkness. There's a hole inside of me, an emptiness that burns me to the core. I fear giving up is my only hope. –

As I struggle between good and evil, I suddenly become consumed with desire and hope. At this moment, my feelings become very clear. One day at a time, patience is kind. At the end of the crossroad, the direction is eminent.

The path to redemption is near. To feel serene and secure, I've had a lot to endure. Darkness is then replaced by sunlight. I feel warmth entering my body as the cold bids farewell. I can breathe again…

THE JOURNEY HAS been long since I wrote this piece. The beginning is pretty grim, right? Well, it's the last paragraph you need to look closely at. It's the focus of this chapter. How did I go from despair and darkness to hope and light? It's been a long journey, so let's begin!

I've been battling depression and anxiety pretty much my whole life. I've reached rock bottom more times that I care to admit. One day, I woke up and felt I'd had an epiphany. I was fed up, and I didn't want to feel this way anymore. I wanted my life back! In that moment, I looked depression and anxiety right in the eye and shouted off at the top of my lungs, "I'm breaking up with you!" That's when the journey to redemption began…

There Is No Shame In Asking For Help.

First things first! You have to start somewhere, so I saw my doctor, and I was given medication to help with my serotonin imbalance. Yes, it's a medical condition! Each condition is unique and has different triggers. Some of you may not believe in or condone taking antidepressants, and some may not need them, but for me, in the same, would you deny a diabetic their insulin?

I knew this was not the only course of action, so I sought the help of a Registered Psychotherapist & Cognitive Behavioral Therapist (Christine Rioux). It was also suggested that I seek the help of an Occupational Therapist (Elnaz Saleh). These two amazing ladies were rays of sunshine during those dark moments. With their help, we set goals and designed an action plan. I was ready!

"Health Is A State Of Body. Wellness Is A State Of Being."
~ J. Stanford

Most people know that exercise is good for your physical health, but it is also good for your mental health. I'm not a big fan of aerobics and all that high impact stuff. You know what I'm talking about, right? The one where the girls pop out of your bra, and end up smacking you in the face with every jump, so you wake up with a black eye the next day! I opted for yoga. It's a little safer. If you're not into exercise or sports, you can try dance classes. I took a Bollywood Dance class once. Believe me, it's quite the workout! I may not be the most coordinated, but I had a lot of fun. Music is known to soothe the soul, and it can help lift your spirits when you're feeling down. It's magical! Like Justin Timberlake sings; "Can't Stop the Feeling!" So, go ahead, and get your groove on! I also started meditating and breathing exercises. Breathing… Can you imagine trying to practice deep breathing when you're so used to shallow breathing. Wow! Dizzy spells! Am I drunk? Am I having a heart attack? I persevered! When you actually get used to it, it's extremely beneficial. It helps with mental clarity, relaxation, dealing with difficult situations, stress, etc.

Positive Mind. Positive Vibes. Positive Life.

Next, I had the guts to try positive thinking. Now that's a hard one when you've felt your whole life that you were a screw up, that there was something wrong with you, and that the world was against you.

I started putting sticky notes all over my apartment. I wrote messages on my mirrors. Little messages like: you are beautiful, you have value, you are amazing, you have a place here. I also printed inspirational messages from the Internet, and would hang them on my refrigerator. You get the idea. Seeing these day after day after day, it starts to sink in. I had a boost of energy and my ego was getting big!

Some of them were funny, but the one that stands out to me, and is still hung in my cubicle at the office and at home is my Taser one. One day, I was so discouraged and frustrated with people that I had a bit of a meltdown. You know that moment when someone tells you something that infuriates you so much that you feel like you are going to blow a gasket, or your head will explode.

Depression and anxiety plagues you with a lot of negative emotions like frustration and anger because of all the pain. You are overwhelmed by emotional pain as well as physical pain. It can become debilitating if you let it get to you, so finding ways to express your emotions in a more positive way can sometimes be a challenge, but it can be done. With the help of my Psychotherapist, we worked together to find ways to help cope with the negative emotions.

Mental image is everything, especially when you feel like you are about to lose it. Now, on to the rest of my story: That day, I was so consumed by my emotions that I started searching online for a Taser gun. Yes, I went there! I soon realized that they were illegal in Canada. What to do? I was not going to break the law, and I certainly did not want to end up behind bars! I started thinking of the series "Orange Is the New Black" and I was freaking out! I look awful in orange! Of course, I was just being silly, and trying to make light of a dark moment. I decided to focus on a mental image. I created a poster, and on it I wrote; "This is a Taser moment!", and added the picture of a nice pink Taser right in the middle. Now every time negative emotions try to consume me, I get this image in my head of the Taser, and my inside voice starts laughing. Then, I can just brush that moment off and move on with my day with a smile. It's a lot safer and fully legal! Oops! I just realized that now everyone knows my secret! Laughing out loud! Oh! And laughter is a miracle cure as well, so it's ok to be silly at times, and have fun. If I was a doctor, I would prescribe it to all my patients. It's proven to be very effective. It just works!

"Journal Writing Is A Voyage Of The Interior."
~ Christina Baldwin

Journaling is where you can write your experiences - like what you've been through, how you felt, what you did, etc. It puts things in perspective, and you realize that you have options and solutions exist. You will also see your accomplishments, and that will make you realize that it's not all gloomy. To see your progress on paper will give you a boost that will motivate you to continue on. There will be ups and downs, but try to concentrate on the positive. This is what will guide you.

Dip Into Your Own Soul. Find Your Truth. What Calls To Your Heart. What Moves Your Spirit. Make Your Life Dance To The Song Of Your Own Essence.

Now this one, I'm going to tackle with white gloves on. Yes, I will be talking spirituality. Not religion, but spirituality. There is a difference. I read on the Internet this inspirational quote, and it sums it up very well; "Religion is belief in someone else's experience. Spirituality is having your own experience". It all started when I decided to go see an Energy Healer. I met Monica Dumont through a Meetup group. I went to her home one night for a meditation session. She introduced me to energy healing and it opened up a whole new world for me.

I discovered this sense of inner peace that I had never felt before.

Emotions and spirituality are linked. Having something to believe in, gives you a sense of belonging and you don't feel so alone anymore. It gives life meaning and purpose. The fear dissipates. I felt empowered and liberated from suffering.

"Books Are The Quietest And Most Constant Of Friends;
They Are The Most Accessible And Wisest Of Counselors,
And The Most Patient Of Teachers." ~ Charles William Eliot

A self-help book is written with the intent to instruct its readers on solving personal problems. I'm not going to go into details on this one because you already know what I'm talking about since you are reading this book. Good for you! It works! I've quoted a few in this chapter.

People Inspire You, Or They Drain You – Pick Them Wisely.

In our everyday life, we are surrounded by people. Some are a joy to be around, and others just drain us of our energy. That's why it's important to surround yourself with positive people. You don't need the drama or negativity. Speak up! It's ok to say no. Be assertive! Of course, always be polite and respectful in doing so. The people who don't respect you, shouldn't be in your life. Some people are triggers to negative experiences in your life. Find healthier people! By that, I mean those who encourage and support you. The ones who will be there, no matter what and who accept you just the way you are without judgement.

With Brave Wings, She Flies.

Last, but certainly not least and the most important for me is putting yourself out there. I truly believed that I was alone. I felt worthless, ashamed and was afraid of being judged. Most of all, I was scared! This is a quote that really helped me along the way, "REMEMBER: There's never been a person in history who was universally loved by everyone, so don't waste your time with the IMPOSSIBLE goal. Be yourself and you'll attract like-minded people." From the book, *Assertiveness For Earth Angels*, by Doreen Virtue. I read this one on the Internet, and it's my favorite; it's ok if some people don't like you. Not everybody has good taste. Brené Brown also mentioned in her book, *Wholehearted Living,* "The risk of losing myself feels more dangerous than the risk of letting people see the real me." So, one day I opened a Facebook account, and I decided it was time to go public about my struggles with depression and anxiety. What helped me face this fear was the day I saw a video of Kristen Bell, the actress and singer. She had gone public, and shared her struggles with depression and anxiety. What resonated with me was when she said that there is nothing weak about struggling with mental illness. Her courage made me realize that I could do this and needed to do this. I wanted to face my fear. Well, let me tell you that I'm so thankful for her, because the day I posted my struggles on Facebook, I got nothing but support from other people going through similar situations. Even people who weren't struggling with this, were reaching out. I wasn't alone anymore. I made friends, and realized that there was absolutely nothing wrong with me. I had a medical condition, yes; but it did not define me. I felt so free! I finally got rid of all the chains that were holding me back! This was definitely a breakthrough!

The main message that comes out of all this, is that most of what you are going through, you yourself create it in your mind. **PERCEPTION!** I've read many definitions on what perception is, but one thing that stood out in most of them is the word conscious. You have a conscious choice! So, consciously choose the light instead of the darkness. Once you fill your mind with positivity, and you get to the crossroad, you will know which way you need to go. Yes, there will be bumps along the way, but you will keep going. You are resilient! Like my Occupational Therapist once told me; "You are like a train. There's been stops along the way, some longer than others, but you keep going. Even on darker days, you have a glow. You never give up!"

Throughout all this, never forget to give thanks. Gratitude is healing. Show gratitude for the good moments because there will be some. It's never all bad! No matter what steps you decide to take in order to get on the road to redemption, gratitude will let you see the situation in a more positive way, and open up your thinking to new solutions. It will make your day worthwhile.

In conclusion, if you want to do this, you can! It is within you! Sometimes, you have to reach into the depths of your soul to find it, but it's there. You owe it to yourself! You have been in the shadows for way too long. It is time for you to shine! So, go ahead, and perceive yourself into the peaceful, positive and amazing life you so deserve! You are worth it! Most of all, remember to smile! It's infectious! If you're not careful, you will catch it!

Chapter 12

Sometimes, We Make Up Stories In Our Own Head.

by Kimberly Francis, RN

"I have lived a long life and had many troubles, most of which never happened."

~ Mark Twain

Kimberly Francis

Kimberly Francis is a health and wellness Network Marketing Entrepreneur, coauthor, leader and personal coach where she helps people get unstuck and be unstoppable in many areas in their life.

She began her career as a Registered Nurse working in critical care before her injury that left her wondering what life was going to throw at her next. Finding a passion living a non- toxic lifestyle, Kimberly began to build a flourishing business that has allowed her to find gratitude, realizing she was meant for so much more in life.

A speaker in her community, Kimberly educates people to live a more natural lifestyle. She is sought after for her fun and entertaining groups where she mentors leaders in her industry, driving them to chase their dreams and succeed in their organization.

A native Rhode Islander, Kimberly is a mom of 3, wife and avid reader. She loves being around people having fun, sharing memories and laughing. Living out her passion on her terms has given her an increased excitement for a renewed endeavour believing anything is possible. Kimberly loves to travel, enjoys spending time at the beach and sharing her love of writing through her Blog.

fb: facebook.com/KimberlyFrancisRN
www.kimberlyfrancisrn.com

I GREW UP in a household where I was told to never rely on anyone. Work hard, go to school, get a job, retire, and die. I felt like I was meant for so much more in life; this couldn't be all that life had to offer... could it? Why did I feel there was so much more? Everyone thought this was the American dream; an incredible job as a Registered Nurse, three beautiful children, a wonderful husband and picture perfect home. I should have been completely fulfilled, right? WRONG! There was something missing, but what? Inside, I desired more...

I Think God Heard Me

God was definitely listening the day I walked into the ICU for work. Don't get me wrong; I love helping others, I just wasn't happy to be there anymore. Like so many other jobs, there just becomes a point where you feel as if you are not appreciated any longer. The field of nursing, especially in the Intensive Care Unit, invokes a constant battle that pulls directly at the heart and soul. Within an hour of being on my shift, a patient threw me across the room, resulting in a herniation of several discs in my back. The pain was unbearable; I initially had little hope to be able to get back on my feet again. How was I going to live the last part of my life? I was in so much pain, God take me now. I knew I couldn't give up so easily; my family needed me to be strong. Therapy, surgery, and more therapy... frankly, I didn't know where to turn next. Why did God do this to me?

Enough

So now what...? I was in pain, depressed and living with no passion in my soul. Having so many feelings raging through me all at once, anxiety, worthlessness, aggravation, I became a different person. My kids got the short end of the stick; I couldn't run, bike or play and my attitude sucked.

God let me suffer, and it was my entire fault.

The story I was telling the universe didn't
match what I truly wanted.

Negativity ran rampant through my mind at all times, I couldn't escape
it. Despite my numerous accomplishments, I continually made up
stories about how inadequate I was. That became my way of life until
one day, I truly had ENOUGH! I threw a SHIT FIT! Seriously, I need
to go to the hospital shit fit. I couldn't do it anymore. That experience
alone opened my eyes; I couldn't live like this anymore.

There Was Another Plan

As a nurse, traditional western medicine was all I knew. I worked in a
culture where if something went wrong, you take a pill. Despite that
belief, it just wasn't cutting it anymore; the constant habit of taking pill
after pill had me trapped in my own body. Frankly, I tried everything I
knew of: a pain specialist, therapy, acupuncture, chiropractor and more
medication. Nothing was helping, I couldn't find any alternative... was
this ever going to end?

A friend kept posting on social media how she started using these
products to support her body systems. These products are all natural,
non-toxic, and have been used for centuries for muscular and emotional
support.... WHAT? How have I not heard of this? After getting the
gist of things, I immediately ordered the whole kit. What did I have
to lose anyway? I was intrigued. That one encounter was the beginning
of my journey into the world of eastern medicine, a place where a new
sense of relief suddenly overwhelmed me.

It was amazing. I couldn't believe using the products and applying
these strategies would renew my enthusiasm for life. I found a passion

for something new, so I focused a business around health and wellness products. Something I'll be able to empower others with. This wasn't just about a product, but a lifestyle. The lifestyle in itself inspired me to share it with others.

Empowerment

There became a point in this new journey where it started to evolve into my everyday lifestyle. The first step was to start living in the present moment, "Right Here, Right Now." I started listening to my whole body. I was aware of all my senses, I started paying attention on purpose and I became mindful of my surroundings. This wasn't the easiest, but finally there was a place for me to start from. Focusing on health and being well was my new priority; I had a new sense of life discovery that needed to be shared. I definitely knew I wasn't going to be perfect, so I decided to be *perfectly imperfect* which was better than what I was before. Beginning to focus on my new way of life, I provided my body with natural benefits and purified my environment daily. I felt empowered; Honestly, I couldn't believe the changes it made for me emotionally. The more I listened to my senses, the more I started respecting myself. Sharing my vision came effortlessly. Everything was a struggle in the beginning, however I knew that I had something special here. Coming up with a plan, I focused my efforts into designing my life to correspond with specific and achievable goals in the short and long term.

Gratitude

That being said, I had it all wrong. I repeatedly sought out the material things I thought made me happy. I was grateful for the nice purse and expensive car. Then came new pair of shoes and designer jeans. I kept seeking out the next THING I thought made me happy, but in fact,

TRUE gratitude comes from the blessings that are directly in front of you every day.

Gratitude is simply the expression of thankfulness; it is an act of humility, recognition of good, and blessings in one's life. Well, guess what? It took me a very long time to feel TRUE gratitude. It took work. Despite the necessary efforts, this was by far the most important discovery of my life.

I wrote it down in my own personal gratitude journal; blessings in my life that I never previously opened my eyes to. I took everything for granted: my family, friends, and health. Now every day before I go to bed, I write down three things that I appreciated most during the day. It could be as simple as your kids not fighting during breakfast. As I read through my journal, it brings joy to my heart how I now can find gratitude in every area of my life.

Make The Decision

For so many years I thought negatively; I spoke in the negative and my energy remained in a negative space. Did I really want to remain in this universe of negative energy? Hell No! I made the decision to start speaking with affirmations. With faith in the future, one is able to free yourself from the negative things in life.

It was time to change my thoughts and life for the better. Becoming clear with my intentions and writing them down was essential. Having these intentions, it was much easier to speak in the positive; "I am," compared to "I wish," or "I want." I had faith in what the universe was going to provide. I made the decision to believe in myself. Whenever I had pain, I said, "I feel better every day;" this compared to "will I ever get rid of this pain?" Get it? You and only you need to make the decision to surround yourself with positive words and have faith in the universe.

It's Time To Grow

When I started my business, the first thing I was taught was to make goals. Although goals are important when starting a business, it is imperative to keep in mind not only the destination, but also the lifelong journey. For my journey, it was my time to serve others. I was hungry for knowledge, culture and growth. I wanted to give to others in the same capacity that I was served. I felt blessed that such a wonderful opportunity was given to me, but I was never going to forget where I came from. It pushes me out of my comfort zone *EVERYDAY* and leaves me wanting more.

In life, growth is the only guarantee that tomorrow is going to get better. In terms of personal growth, intentions are absolutely key to keeping you on track each and every day of the week. Intentions allow us to stay on the path to personal success. Personal growth is a lifelong journey to fulfill your potential. So many of us are anxious to improve our situation, but refuse to improve ourselves. Working hard doesn't guarantee success. Focusing on your growth with clarity and being disciplined in your strategies determines the height of your personal growth.

Take Action

It is so damn easy to say all of this, but putting it all together into a plan was another story. I knew what I needed to do to change my way of life; I needed to move in a more positive direction and be the person I always envisioned. So I decided I needed to take some action.

I couldn't give myself value if I didn't see
the value in myself.

Right? So every day, I took my journal even if I thought I had nothing to be grateful for that day and I wrote.

I began to grow my business. I knew I loved the process and I was building an incredible organization. Finding a passion enabled me to feel better not only physically, but also emotionally. The process of sharing eastern practices to empower families to stay healthy and live in wellness is so vital to me. Is this what I have been missing? I found an enthusiasm for waking up each day and helping others build a team for themselves through networking and values.

Nothing Is Impossible

Each day, it became clearer that this is where I was meant to be. The pain, depression, anxiety and worry that I used to feel on a daily basis was no longer in control of me. I started to embrace my life by guiding my internal and external pressures while on the way to success. I broke down IMPOSSIBLE to I'M POSSIBLE! There was so much more to life; the universe put together a completely new plan for me, and I was ready to go out into the world and deliver it.

Kick Stress In The Ass

Don't ever settle. There is so much more in life… only when you fall as deep as possible, do you realize that enough is enough. It is now time to look a little deeper and ask those serious questions. What do I really want in my life? Why do I want it? Most people don't know the answers to these questions; you must sit down with those who are closest to you to begin the process of finding out what really matters most.

For me, I wanted to help others; working in a community hospital was not my American dream. It was something deeper. Without God pushing me to the end, my passion would have never been found.

My days of living someone else's vision of a perfect life would have remained until I retired and died. Wake up and kick stress in the ass. It is time to sing your song. Be grateful for your talents, have faith in what the universe has in store for you and take some serious action. If you want to start your own business, no matter what anyone says, *do it*. If you want to become a personal trainer, *do it*. If you want to go back to school and change careers, *do it*. Staying where you are will just continue the cycle of self-doubt. It's our time to live on our terms and it's scary. Growing is scary, but living your life inconsistent with your values is terrifying. Most of our life is getting to the destination. We need to remember to enjoy the journey through the challenges and the triumphs; you'll discover the joy of your own happiness in the end.

Chapter 13

My Way Back To Health

by Amanda Yeatman

"One cannot think well, love well, sleep well, if one has not dined well."
~ Virginia Woolf

Amanda Yeatman

Amanda Yeatman, an adventurist, nature lover, and an optimist who believes with passion that life can be anything and everything you ever dreamed it could be, you just have to be brave; don't be afraid of change or failure, lead with love in your heart and see the world through a child's eye: full of beauty, opportunity, and wonder. Amanda started travelling right after High School. She travelled throughout Western Canada, Europe, parts of the United States, and then to India on a mission trip to immunize children for Polio. She then moved back to her home town where she opened a Café at the young age of 21. She then headed back out West to Calgary where she lives now and became a mother to three incredible children. Her children, Avrey, Emma, and Sadie have filled her heart and soul with so much joy and love. Health and nutrition became a large focus for Amanda after having children. She knew that in order to keep her mind, body and soul fit, she needed to work every day on eating well, being physically active, centering her mind through meditation, and living her own authentic, inspired life. Amanda studied at the Institute for Integrative Nutrition – a well-rounded education based on Nutrition & Holistic Health. Amanda knew that it was her mission to share what she had learned on her own journey to wellness with others, so she started an Integrative Health Coaching practice. Her Health Coaching practice focuses on helping others find their authentic selves through full circle lifestyle health. In her practice, she works with clients on trying to find balance in everything from Nutrition, Career, Spirituality, Home Environment, Joy, Relationships, Physical Activity, Connecting with Nature, Home Cooking, and so much more. Amanda plans to continue her education and become a Registered Massage Therapist and Yoga instructor. Amanda dreams big, lives big, and loves big and encourages everyone to do the same.

AmandaYeatmanWellness@gmail.com
fb: @AmandaYeatmanWellness

FOOD IS ONE of life's beautiful pleasures and should be prepared and enjoyed as such. But life is busy and we run out of time to even think about eating well. We have developed into not only a fast paced, but also a fast food nation. Every corner has a drive through, we can get delivery from just about anywhere, we've got instant this-instant that and meal-in-a-bag solutions that we eat at our desks, in our cars, and scarf down quickly as we rush from one meeting to another. Putting aside for a moment that these fast food solutions are depleted of any quality nutrients, think about how much *more* stress we put on our bodies when we eat this way. And yet we wonder why we are plagued with a huge population of people struggling with digestive illnesses and chronic diseases? We very well may have forgotten the importance of quality food and taking the time to think about what we eat and how we eat it. Instead, we just eat for the sake of eating instead of eating to nourish, fuel, and revitalize our body, mind, and soul.

Eating well has become such a focus in my life. It never used to be. I used to fill up on all the wrong junk foods and eat only a small amount of what I knew I should be eating like fruits, vegetables, quality proteins, and whole grains. This didn't affect me as much, that I could see, when I was younger but once I started getting older, having children, and as the years went on, I realized that I just didn't *feel* right, I didn't *feel* good. I wasn't hugely overweight but I had been carrying around a few extra pounds that I just could not lose. The number on the scale was not the biggest issue. The big issue was how I felt. I wanted to feel light, energized, and glowing. But, instead, I felt tired, foggy, my skin was breaking out, my eczema seemed to be getting worse, and I had very intense highs and lows. I didn't realize until later that my diet played such a big role in all of it.

My skin was a big indicator that something wasn't quite right with me. I was breaking out and then I was diagnosed with rosacea. Along with my skin and the extra weight, I would look in the mirror and think to myself, "This isn't who I want to be. This isn't the healthy, sexy, strong, ambitious, mother and woman I want to be. The trouble was, I didn't have the strength in my body or the clarity in my mind to figure out how to get my health back on track.

It was once I started researching solutions for my rosacea, that I found the true connection between diet and health. I could have gone to the doctor and been given a prescription for my symptoms but that didn't feel right to me. There had to be a more natural way. Through the research I did, I began to see that we can cure ourselves of so many illnesses and find our way back to health just through what we eat. This "theory" was solidified later once I became a holistic health practitioner. So, with that in mind, it was simple, I began to change what I ate. I added in more greens, vegetables, whole grains, fruits, quality proteins, more alkaline forming foods, and I took out the acidic, over processed, preservative ridden, artificial foods. With simply doing that, I saw an incredible difference. My skin started to clear up, I began to feel energized, focused, centered, and healthy. My mood was more stable, the extra weight was coming off, and my sugar cravings subsided. I felt amazing!

One day, I came across this Holistic Health school. I thought it looked very interesting because I now wanted to know everything about nutrition! The school was all about how our diet affects our health; our mind, body, and soul. The education was enthralling! It was eye opening! It was all about clean, wholesome nutrition, and finding the right foods for your body. It was also about finding health through career, creativity, joy, and spiritual practice. It was exactly what I needed. I had started eating well but aligning my life choices and hobbies around being healthy was the necessary step I needed to think about. The school taught me to find a connection to myself, listen to my body, and to make health a priority. These lessons resonated with me. I applied my learnings and became more authentic, and mindful of my life choices, my body, and my mind.

As time went on and I continued my studies and continued to

apply what I had learned, I was absolutely astounded by the changes in my health. I felt so amazing! I wanted to scream it from the rooftops! I do still have to work on my health being a primary focus in my life every day and when life gets busy and I don't make time to prepare and eat heathy meals or I miss my workouts and meditations, I feel it. I know that if I went back to not eating well, not exercising, not making time for the things I love to do, and not doing my meditations, I would feel depressed, tired, and scattered. Almost daily, I remind myself of this. I focus my intentions on making my health a priority. I know that if I don't have my health, I can't be successful in my endeavors, and I can't be the mother, woman, friend, and partner I want to be.

The biggest lesson I have learned these last few years is that food heals. It heals your body, and heals your soul. And what you eat matters. "Let food be thy medicine" – Hippocrates. How true.

Food changed me. It cured me. I am a work in progress, but I can say that I have changed my entire body, mind, and attitude by just changing what I eat.

I know that there are so many illnesses out there that can be cured and even prevented by focusing on what we eat.

I have become almost the very best version of myself (always room for a little more improvement). I meditate daily, I exercise daily, and I am very aware of what foods are going into my body and how those foods are making me feel. And, by no means am I starving or denying myself of any pleasures. I still indulge! I have found a way to make good healthy food, vibrant, flavorful, satisfying, and delicious! I eat foods that keep my body fit and my mind focused. I've had to work at experimenting with food by cooking more at home, trying different recipes and learning to cook with new foods. Making time to get in the kitchen was one of the most important steps to finding my way back to health.

A concept of healthy eating I have tried to adopt is the idea of living off the land. Now, I am not suggesting that we should all go out and buy a farm and get to work, but what if we adopted this way of thinking about what we eat? So, living off the land would mean eating fresh organic fruit, vegetables, greens, free range organic protein, eggs, all homemade meals, and eating only foods in season. Plus, this would mean adopting a much slower, less stressed pace around eating, taking the time to prepare our meals, and then enjoying the meal with gratitude and joy.

Here are some tips to start you on your journey to finding your way back to health and making wholesome food the centerpiece in your life.

Have Fun In The Kitchen

Make it fun! Light a candle, turn on some music, let your mind relax and just start cooking. Cooking can be a great stress release. Focus on cooking with love and gratitude, you'll taste the difference! Spend a little time checking out recipes and intriguing meal ideas. Plan and prepare. Try and cut back on fast food consumption and put more time into planning, preparing, and organizing your meals. At first, I was not keen on the idea that I was going to have to spend time meal planning or preparing, but then I quickly realized that if there was nothing healthy and easy to grab in the house, I would never make good food choices. Choose one day a week that you get into the kitchen and cook! Do some make ahead, cut, dice, marinate. Put some effort into it. Remember, rarely do we *have the time*, it is all about *making the time*. Eating well does not necessarily mean all gourmet all the time. Easy, quick to make, healthy meals are just as good. Find your time to be in the kitchen. I find I like to be in the kitchen in the morning. I get up a little earlier and I plan out dinner, do any make ahead preparations I can, I get my lunch ready for the day and if I still have a bit of time, I throw in a batch of muffins! Find the time of day that feels right for you to be in the kitchen.

Be Mindful Of What You Are Eating

Sit down for your meals, try closing your eyes for a moment, truly taste it. Savor it, show gratitude for what you are eating and appreciate yourself for the effort you made to prepare that meal. Invite friends to share the food with, spread the love, enjoy the meal together. Try not to eat your main meals on the go or in front of the television or while working. Make it a priority to eat slowly, breathe, and enjoy.

Exercise & Meditate. Find Your Spiritual Connection

Find an exercise that works for you. Try out some new classes, try cardio, yoga, zumba, pilates, swimming, cycling, and see what works for you. Make exercise a priority in your life. Find a spiritual connection that works for you. Whether it is your religion, or maybe it's connecting with nature, or maybe it's meditation. Whatever your spiritual practice is, make it a priority in your life.

Add In The Good Stuff & Take Out The Bad

Adding in a significant amount of greens and vegetables is a huge part of eating well. I used to think that one garden salad was enough, but then I realized, my body needed so much more chlorophyll which is found in dark, green, leafy vegetables. Get your greens in! Have a green smoothie in the morning, steamed kale or sautéed spinach with your eggs, salmon, or pasta. Try some collard greens and Swiss chard. Try some romaine lettuce cups filled with steamed rice, sautéed peppers, onions, garlic, mushrooms and salsa. At the grocery store, fill up in the produce aisle. Make vegetables and fruit your go to snacks. Make sure your plate is bursting with color at meal times. Stay away from the boxed, processed goods. Read the label. If you see these ingredients on the label, put it back! Carrageenan, Caramel Color, Artificial Sweeteners, Trans Fat, Sugar, Monosodium Glutamate, High-Fructose Corn Syrup, Palm Oil, Shortening, Processed "White" Foods (white bagels, bread, rice). Instead, opt for 100 percent whole grains. Corn Syrup, Sodium Benzoate, Potassium Benzoate, Butylated Hydroxyanisole (BHA), Sodium Nitrates, Sodium Nitrites (processed meats), Blue, Green, Red, Yellow (anything with a color or number is artificial), MSG. I know there is a lot of talk around dairy and whether our bodies can properly digest it, but I believe that we are all different and we need to listen to how our bodies react to certain foods. What works for one person may not work for another. I was dairy free for quite a few years after having my son but later I introduced high-quality organic cheese back into my diet and it has worked well for me. Experiment with how you feel after a small amount of dairy and if it doesn't feel right in your body, take it off the menu. If you are eating dairy, opt to have it as a very small portion of your meals. Experiment with how meat works with your body. I eat eggs and fish, but I stay away from other meats because they don't work well in my body. See what works for you. If you are opting to eat meat, go for organic, grass-fed. Try some superfoods like acai, chia seeds, quinoa, goji berries, Cacao Powder/Cocoa Powder, Maca Powder, Seaweed, Kefir, Hemp Seeds, Chaga Mushrooms.

Here is a list of some great foods to add in to your diet. As an exercise, circle the foods that you have eaten in the last couple of days, and then find a few foods on the list that you can start adding into your diet today!

Celery, Oranges Grapefruit, Lemons, Tangerines, Red Bell

Peppers, Broccoli, Garlic, Ginger, Spinach, Yogurt, Kiwi, Sunflower Seeds, Acai Berry, Oysters, Chia Seeds, Quinoa, Sweet Potato, Mushrooms, Almond Butter, Peanut Butter, Cashew Butter, Raw Almonds, Pistachios, Beans, Lentils, Sesame Seeds, Brown Rice, Honey, Banana, Carrots, Eggs, Snap Peas, Kale, Olive Oil, Watermelon, Green Tea, Avocado, Oats, Grapes, Brussel Sprout, Asparagus, Swiss Chard, Blueberries, Pistachios, Wild-Caught Alaskan Salmon, Dark Chocolate, Organic Turkey breast, Organic Chicken, Grass-fed Beef, Walnuts, Oranges, Chickpeas, Coconut.

Here are a few quick and simple recipes to try!

Quick & Easy Quiche
6 Free Range Organic Eggs
1/4 cup of Milk
1 ½ cup of Spinach
1 tablespoon of diced Onion
1-2 Garlic cloves
1/3 cup of grated Swiss cheese
Salt & Pepper

Preheat oven to 350F. Sauté onions and garlic in a pan until soft, add spinach until soft. Mix together eggs, milk and cheese. I use the pre-made pie crust. Bake shell for 10 minutes until edges are golden brown. Let it cool. Mix sautéed onions, spinach, and garlic into eggs, add salt and pepper. Pour into cooled pie shell and bake for 30-35 minutes (until eggs are fully cooked) Serve with a mixed green salad and, voila! You've got lunch for the next 3 days!

Peanut Butter Power Balls

2/3 cup Oats

1/3 cup Peanut butter

1 tbsp Chia seeds

1 tbsp Coconut

1 tablespoon of Honey

Roll into balls and chill for 30 minutes in fridge.

Yogurt Power Bowl

½ a cup of Yogurt *

I use cultured unsweetened coconut yogurt but you can use organic plain as well. Best to look for organic probiotic yogurt that is not loaded with sugar.

Top with Raspberries, Strawberries, or Blueberries

Unsweetened shredded Coconut

Cinnamon

Sliced Almonds (you can use Walnuts or Pecans if you prefer)

Chia seeds

Pumpkin seeds

Try this power bowl as a topping for your oatmeal too! If you need a bit more sweetness, drizzle some pure maple syrup or honey on top.

Veggie Hummus Wrap
Hummus
Tzatziki
Sliced Cucumber
Sliced Tomato
Cheese of your choice (I use Swiss or Feta)
Romaine Lettuce or Spinach
Diced Green or Red Pepper
1 Whole grain Tortilla

Spread hummus and tzatziki all over tortilla, add diced veggies and romaine lettuce, top with feta cheese, Swiss, or cheddar whatever you prefer. Wrap up and go!

I focus on making my health a priority in my life and living each day with gratitude, for I have found my way. I hope by making your health a primary focus in your life, and by applying the tips in this chapter, you can find your way back to health too.

Come visit my page for recipes, health tips, coaching services, and more!
FB: @AmandaYeatmanWellness

Section 4

— ◆ ✂ ◆ —

More Than Just A Girl

featuring

Dr. Supriya Gade, Michelle Zubrinich and Rusiana T Mannarino.

Editorial commentary by Ky-Lee Hanson

ALMOST DAILY, WE hear of absurd and completely unacceptable behavior. As women, we face more external pressures than our male counterparts. Is that fair to say? Men have their share of expectations. Men of color have an extremely unfair stereotype. As women, we are sensitive to this. However, men structured our society. Women, for a long time, were lesser of the two.

Women of the 1600's wore high-heeled shoes to be equal to men and in the mid 19th-century, pornography brought back heels as a sex symbol. [1] We have since been turning heels into a power statement but until 2015, women were required to wear heels and short skirts in many restaurants across North America. When it is not a choice but an expectation, it is sexist. As of late, women have choice in their work attire and exercise that freedom.

We live our lives hearing cat calls and sexist remarks. We carry pepper spray but are afraid to use it because if he did not lay a hand yet, we are labelled an attacker. If a female is drunk, many courts do not see rape, as rape. Even if the attacker drags her behind a dumpster and does as he pleases to her unconscious body without consent, his sentence could be lessened due to alcohol involvement and his social status. [2] Commonly, if she was drunk and he sexually assaulted her, he is not as guilty in the eyes of many.

So far, we have talked about self-love, balance and health. This will help us to alleviate internal pressures but together as women, we need to stand. We need to share our pain and bring forward what is wrong. We need to be vocal and support one another. Next, Dr. Supriya Gade, Michelle Zubrinich and Rusiana T. Mannarino do just that by sharing how to establish boundaries, stand up for ourselves firmly, and break the proverbial glass ceiling socio-culturally, and professionally.

---

[1] Wade,L.(2013, February 5). From Manly to Sexy: The History of the High Heel. Retrieved from The Society Pages Online. https://thesocietypages.org/socimages/2013/02/05/from-manly-to-sexy-the-history-of-the-high-heel/

[2] Gore, W. (2016, June 10). Why Brock Turner is not actually a rapist: Around the world outraged headlines have referred to the 'Brock Turner rape case. Retrieved from The Independent http://www.independent.co.uk/voices/stanford-rape-case-brock-turner-victims-statement-a7074246.html

Chapter 14

Overcoming Stereotype
Fitting Is Boring. Be Fiercely You.

by Dr. Supriya Gade

"Your time is limited, so don't waste it living someone else's life. Don't be
trapped by dogma- which is living the results of other people's thinking.
Don't let the noise of others' opinions drown out your own inner voice.
And most importantly, have the courage to follow your heart and intuition.
They somehow already know what you truly want to become."

~ Steve Jobs

Dr. Supriya Gade

Supriya Gade, a professional by day, an artist by night, and a dreamer throughout. She is a physician by background and is currently a doctoral candidate for Healthcare Administration Program with Central Michigan University. She has dedicated her life to empowering everyone around her to make their life a little better - one step at a time. In the professional sphere, she simply does it by helping to improve the quality of healthcare service delivery. In her personal sphere, she does it by being a big sister, a good friend, a loving wife and just being herself through her blogs and poetries.

She was born into a typical, traditional, middle-class, Indian household where being a woman meant fulfilling societal norms at all costs. Moving beyond that paradigm and in true search of self-expression, she has established herself as a successful professional in the healthcare field. Her life journey has taken her from Mumbai to Houston TX, to Windsor ON, before finally settling down in Toronto. Making most out of her experiences and her expertise, she runs a business consultancy on the side, helping non-profit organizations with their operations. She is also a co-founder of a personal coaching business that she manages with her husband.

An Indian by heart and a Canadian in the making, she embodies the essence of both – freedom and enlightenment!

Business Consulting @ www.fourdisciplines.com
Personal Coaching @ www.rohitraaman.com

Obedient Daughter

It was a sunny and bright morning in Toronto. Exactly matching my state of mind. It was going to be one of those important days when I realized my dreams one inch at a time. Waking up in my ever so loving husband's arms, in my humble abode with full vitality and health, and having a job that I felt grateful for… I was just counting my blessing when the phone rang. It was a late evening in India and the perfect time for my mother to have her evening (and for me morning) chitchat. Call me impatient, but I could not wait longer. I was hoping for formal paper in my hands today to disclose the news to parents.

But I gave in and blurted, "Hey mom, guess what I just got promoted - awesome title and a great salary. I am not on contract anymore. It is a full-time deal!"

In a heartbeat, my mom started the parade of questions, "That is nice Supriya. How does Rohit feel about this? What are the timings? Any travel involved?" I knew what my mom was hinting at. I felt the energy draining out of my body. *Not again. Not this conversation again.* I was pulled into a parallel reality where I was a 6-year-old girl in India in my pretty pink dress and two ponytails with red ribbons, sitting on a couch, holding my breath, and listening to my mom's 'mother knows best' speech. In a defensive tone with a hint of courage, I replied, "How does it matter? Can we focus on how good this is for me?"

"No honey, I am happy for you. I really am. Congratulations! I just get worried for you sometimes that may be you don't think these things through. You are in your 30s now. Look at all your friends. Monika has two children age 3 and 5. Wish you were as enthusiastic thinking about babies as these promotions."

Indeed not a great start of the day! By now I am used to such conversations. I had become this agile ninja shifting in and out of these parallel worlds by gently digressing and nudging the discussion in other direction. Though it was disappointing not being able to share my happiness, I brushed it off and went to work. After all, it was my special day!

Amenable She-Boss

At 11 AM team meeting my boss announced my promotion. Everyone at work congratulated me. I basked in my glory as the day progressed.

In a very upbeat mood, I got on to elevator to go to my 2 PM project team meeting. Kirsten and Steve, my team members, also jumped in and we started to chat about the project. I was an acting Project Manager before, but now officially heading this project I was hoping to get quick moves on some of the stalled items. I briefly mentioned how we needed to revisit the specifications with the vendor to hold them accountable for the quality of the product they were delivering.

The elevator door opened, and it should have felt less stuffy, but I could feel the air thickening. Steve looked glassy eyed. Kirsten glanced at him and then at me before providing her valuable two cents, "Hey settle down there. Are you not seriously going to say that to the project team right? I mean if John were to make that decision... he can get away with it. You are just going to sound like a bossy bi**h. Besides, they won't take it seriously". I paused and swallowed the witty remarks that came right to the tip of my tongue. Smiled. And looked for one of my parallel worlds to escape to. Sadly ninja in me was not so swift this time. I let it go... graciously... almost!

Dutiful Wife

Rest of the day was not as eventful. Still happy and upbeat, I wrapped my work after late meetings to rush back home. One should never underestimate Toronto traffic! Sitting in my car, listening to the radio, it must have taken me 40 minutes to cross four lights. And then my car Bluetooth hummed.

It was my aunt from Mumbai. *Something fishy here.* I answered. After exchanging few pleasantries and formal congratulations, not to my surprise, she went right to the heart of the matter. Of course, my mom wanted the aunt to do the bidding for her. My ninja woke straight up, got two double shot coffees and prepared for combat. Ever so swift, it calculated all sorts of tactical scenarios to nudge and digress. *Maybe I should talk about Rohit. She likes him.* "Aunty, I'm driving. It's already late, and I'm rushing home. Rohit is making special celebratory dinner for me. My favorite. Biryani!"

Wish I would have seen this coming.

"That is hilarious. You're driving this late. And your husband is cooking for you as we speak!! When did this go in reverse? I tell you Supriya when you moved to America nine years ago, I asked your parents - who's going show you how to be a good wife. The wholesome Indian values! Sweetheart you can't sustain a marriage like this."

Maybe it was traffic.

Or maybe it was just too many people telling
me how to operate in this world against their
own understanding of all sorts
of stereotypes.

It did get to me this time. I abruptly ended the conversation and hung up. But too late. My stress response was activated. Being a trained physician, I often imagine my body as a simulation model where things happen in a slow motion sequence like how med students learn in their classroom. I could feel my hypothalamic-pituitary-adrenal axis receiving signals to secret cortisol – the stress hormone. *No. This is a happy day. It's no time to be worked up.*

Hmm... A Woman

And then suddenly, there was a bright red light in front of me. The van ahead of me had stopped short. I hit my break as hard as possible. The car behind me didn't. It rammed into me. I jolted. Thankfully not as hard. Recovering from it, I unhooked my seatbelt to come out of the car. The car owner was already marching towards me yelling. Before I could get some words out to say that it's not me who stopped short, the car owner was well into his speech of how f***ing bad this was. "I don't know who gives the driving license to a woman." He must have seen me. As he came closer, he carefully looked at me for a second and continued, "And that too a South Asian one!" I won't list his further sexist and racial comments. But that was it. That was the tipping point of the today. Trying hard to be on the verge of civil, I had few verbal exchanges and left the scene sharing insurance info.

Exhausted from the whole ordeal of the day, I arrived at the parking lot of my condo. Took an elevator to 26th floor. Cortisol had already made his way to all sorts of receptors in my body. The nervous energy was building in. I stepped inside. Rohit was putting finishing touches to his dishes. He gave me an ear to ear smile. Unaware of my day and trying to be playful, he asked, "So, how are you?"

"How am I?", I was just getting started. Cortisol has receptors all over the body. It must have affected my metabolic and homeostatic mechanisms. I briefly recalled my physiology class – Cortisol affects ion transport, the immune response, and even memory. In plain words, rationality was out of the door. My body was ready to fight or flight. Unfortunately, that is a primitive response from the time when caveman (notice man here!) really needed it. At this moment and time, I had no need to fight or flight, but I was pumped. And there was my unaware husband asking me a naïve question!

"How am I? Well, let me start from the top...." My incoherent ranting 15 minutes thereafter contained being fed up of satisfying others' expectation in my life, failing at stereotype tests, feeling not being enough and disappointed and resorting to questioning my own beliefs and potential as a woman.

11 years into the relationship and 9 years into this marriage, Rohit knew what was going on. He just calmly listened to me, holding my hands and waited till the surge of my emotions was over. Exactly the same thing he has been doing a decade long. In many of those early years we had no money, no roof, worked 3 jobs and slept less than 5 hours a day, borrowed money for groceries from our friends, drove a car without air conditioning in the hot Texan summer, had our parents almost denouncing us for inter-caste inter-religion marriage, and moved three countries and four cities to find a place we can finally call home. One thing stayed common: Rohit's patient eyes and easing words.

"Supriya, after all these years, and all the struggle, you chose today to be worked up about it? Aren't you late? The Supriya I know doesn't wait for others to define her. She let these witty ass remarks roll over her back. The Supriya I know does not care about fulfilling racial, gender, ethnic, professional stereotype… mainly woman stereotype… importantly South Asian Indian woman stereotype. You need to stay true to who you really are. You are not a stereotype. You are your own Supriyotype."

By this time, my stress hormones – cortisol, adrenaline, and norepinephrine – were wearing off. Thankfully your body has a mechanism to realize when it's enough. Cortisol travels backward up the relay message system to shut down the stress response – a routine negative feedback.

Supriyotype? Seriously? My sweet husband was just trying to soothe me. And being overly cheesy, yet overly successful in doing so. In no time, I gathered my sense of balance and moved on with my day.

That's my typical life! Okay, maybe not everything happened in same day or in that exact order, but this is the pattern, day in and day out. Don't you feel that every day we are told by someone else what we are supposed to be, and we fight with our own self to be or not to be that person? In small doses, these interferences are disguised as expectation from parents, friends, colleagues or boss, or they could be as sophisticated as general societal norms or quietly polished stereotypes. All of us face this. Women, in particular, more stringently. With glass ceiling and wage difference, would you be surprised?

In simple physics terms, Stress is a measure of the force an object is experiencing per unit cross-sectional area. Breaking stress is the maximum stress a material can stand before it breaks. Simply interpreted in human context, in Supriya's world of definitions, stress is an undue pressure. Pressure or a friction created due to two non-conforming notions. When your notion of yourself is not that of what others expect of you – there is stress!

Aren't you a wee bit irritated when you get stereotyped such as when you're buying a car with your boyfriend/husband and salesman barely talks with you? Or someone automatically assumes just because you're a woman, that you must like fancy fruity alcoholic drinks, romantic comedies, and don't know anything about the sports. More serious assumptions continue - such as - you can't run a successful business unless it has to do with girly things, getting married and having children must be a topmost priority of your life and if you're acting out – it must be because of the 'special days' of the month. These get me seriously irked! My ninja is delirious hopping all these parallel 'realities.' Don't even get me started on more racial-ethnic stereotypes slapped on top of these! With series of these experiences, you constantly find yourself defending against others' notion of you. The stress becomes chronic. So what do we do? How do we break up with stress?

First of all, let's examine where stress come from? The pressure or friction of two non-conforming notions i.e. your version and the world's version. Easy fix - Get rid of the latter! But, can you? Is stereotype always negative? Being of an Indian origin, some might say I'm good with computers. That is a positive characterization. Others might say I'm corrupt and should not be trusted. That is a negative characterization. Being a woman, one might say I'm very nurturing and also might say I'm soft and not assertive. There goes positive and negative characterization again. I would like to be called a computer genius and a nurturing soul, but I do not appreciate those other things said about me.

> The reality is - a characterization of gender, race, and ethnicity is inherent; as that sets us apart in unique identities. When done in bad faith, its mere negative stereotype.

It is very difficult to get rid unless we also sacrifice the positive stereotype at the altar with it.

So, we can't change others or world at large, we don't want to change ourselves in undue influence, then what remains? Maybe there is a solution. We can change our reaction to others and world at large. Can that work? Next time you're subjected to these wise ass remarks, simply listen. Have a conversation with your body. Do not let your hypothalamic axis get triggered for cortisol. Even if you do get stressed, just walk it off. All you need to do is get rid of that nervous energy. Climb few flights of a stairs or throw punches in the air. It will wear off.

What works best is talking with someone who believes in you. In my case, Rohit is that center of gravity. Though other times, he can be a harsh critic; in moments like this, he is my biggest supporter and fan. His sometimes witty, sometimes crazy, and sometimes incredibly mature explanation about the situation brings me down to a comfortable place. Miss Rationality that was booted out of the door, quietly sneaks back on to the couch like nothing has ever happened. Brain and heart function is restored!

Sometimes when he is not available, and I need de-escalation, I look at the entire incident through his lens. Not that my lens is not good; But his is wittier, funnier and wiser. *Don't tell him I said that.* It brings a sort of detachment with it. Because I'm no longer Supriya, but someone else looking at this situation, I'm more objective, and I have different perspective.

In summary, just walk it off, look at it from another lens, or just talk with someone who is your biggest fan. More importantly, don't let it get to you. You don't have to explain yourself to others who can only look from their level of perception. You are too unique to be conformed into the meaningless norms of the stereotypes.

Remember. You are the only original copy of yourself. Now go and show off the true that is you!

Chapter 15

Male Domination, Fuck That.

by Michelle Zubrinich

"This is a man's world, but it wouldn't be nothing,
nothing without a woman or a girl."
~ Betty Jean Newsome (socially referenced as James Brown)

Michelle Zubrinich

Michelle Zubrinich has always been a passionate person who believes that everyone should have a voice. She is tenacious in her businesses and in her pursuit of personal growth, finding joy in everything she does. She grew up in the border town of St.Catharines, Ontario and has called such cities as Paris, France, Montreal, Quebec and currently, Toronto, Ontario, her home.

She has worked in the commercial photography industry since 2008. She tried many different positions in the industry: first, as a lighting assistant, then as a production assistant, followed by a producer, a digital technician and finally found her passion in retouching. It complimented both the creative and technical side of photography that she so enjoyed, which allowed her to run her business from home.

In 2015, Michelle and her husband Rob gave birth to their son Zadak. Although she loves her son more than words can say, there were some very hard and isolating moments during the first couple of months of motherhood. It became clear to her in those days, that she needed a change and wanted to build something bigger than herself. This is when she found Arbonne, which has allowed her to unlock the potential she always knew she had. Her passions for leading and helping others is now fulfilled and there is still so much more to come.

t: @mzubie | ig: @michelle_zub_entrepreneur
mzubie@gmail.com | www.mkzStudios.com

JAMES BROWN CLAIMS to have co-written the song, "This is a man's World," in 1966 with his onetime girlfriend, Betty Jean Newsome. She says that she wrote the lyrics based on her own observations of the relations between the sexes which is ironic because she would also claim that Brown had nothing to do with the writing process and argued in court that he sometimes forgot to pay her royalties. [1] Although much has changed since 1966, we are still not at a point of equality. Currently, women in Canada are paid $.72 on every dollar that men earn. In America, it is broken down even further to show how minority women make even less; Hispanic women earn $.59 to every Caucasian man's dollar, African-American women earn $.60, White women earn $.79 and Asian women earn $.84 to every Caucasian man's dollar. [2] This is caused by a number of different reasons. Traditional "women's work" is seen to be less skilled because it is tied to domestic type of work that women were performing in the home of free. Women make up a large number of part time employment mostly due to inadequate child care options and lack of parental leave. We also account for many lower paid jobs: in Canada, 22% of the Canada's minimum-wage workers in 2009 were women, more than double the proportion of men in the same age group. [3]

We are at a crucial point in history where we are becoming far more aware of the importance of both maternal and paternal influences in the home and there are more men staying home than ever before. There have been many positive steps in the right direction but we are still not where we need to be. Women are still concerned about getting pregnant or not being considered for positions because they are of childbearing age. A woman I know personally, interviewed without her wedding ring because she was in a highly corporate and competitive field and felt that if she were to wear her wedding ring, it could be assumed that she would be having children soon.

These issues are not unique to women who desire to have children. Let's have a look at the tech industry since it seems to be one of the most male dominated industries at the moment. Speak With a Geek, a technology industry recruiter founded in 1999, revealed a shocking study done where they presented an employer with 5,000 resumes. The first time they viewed the resumes, they saw all identifying factors: age, gender, schooling etc. Women accounted for 5% of the people wanted for interviews. They then presented the exact same 5,000 resumes and took away all identifying factors, women accounted for 54% of people who landed interviews. If this doesn't piss you off, I'm not sure what will. And this is nothing new. Researchers at Harvard and Princeton conducted a similar blind interview study in 1970 for the symphony. They found that when blind interviews were conducted, a woman's chance of being hired jumped from 25% to 46 %. [4] So we've made progress in some places but we still have a long way to go.

I was raised with the belief that we are all equal. Race and gender play no role in what you can or can not achieve. Perhaps it is my trusting nature, but it took me a very long time to figure out that not everyone shares this opinion. And with the demonization of the term "feminist" there are still women who believe other women should not be in positions of power. One of my business partners is also a flight attendant. She rarely works with female pilots but there have been a few instances where they have had an all female crew. This has been met with very mixed reviews. One male passenger could not bear the thought of a female flying a plane, so he gave up his seat and got off the plane which was later featured on the news. The other side of the coin is that people stare and point with excitement, but nonetheless, these female pilots are made to feel like animals in a zoo. Our quest for equality is not done until it is not only common but expected to see women in these roles. "You can't be what you can't see" is a very important message in the film, *Miss Representation.*

The demonization of the term feminist is unfortunate. This subject could encompass this whole chapter but I'll reserve that for another time. Some men feel threatened by the term since they assume that it means that women will supersede them and some women feel threatened because they see it as a term that is demeaning towards women who want to stay at home with their families. Neither of these examples are in fact what feminism stands for. It stands for the social and political equality of the sexes.

If you think women should be paid as much as men, you are a feminist. If you think women should be able to vote, you are a feminist. If you think girls should be able to attend school, you are a feminist.

Be A Bad Ass Bitch.

We are in an interesting moment in American history right now since we have the first female running for the Presidency of the United States. I say American history because women in other countries around the world have been in power for many years: Germany, Liberia, Argentina, Bangladesh, Lithuania, Trinidad and Tobago, Brazil, Kosovo, Denmark, Jamaica, South Korea, Slovenia, Norway, Poland and Croatia all currently have female Presidents or Prime Ministers [5]. The 2016 American Presidential campaign has been a brutal circus that has shone a light on the ugliness of people's racism and misogyny. I won't get into the politics of the candidates but what is abundantly clear is that if Donald Trump were running against a man, this election would be a farce. Instead, we have a very unqualified, racist, misogynist man running against an abundantly qualified woman who is being told to smile more; whose wardrobe is being attacked in the media; who's being told she sounds like a "nagging woman" when she is giving her speeches. It is highlighting all the double standards that women face every day. And we do face them. If you are fed up with being given the "pink" files or treated like you are not as smart, strong or quick as a man, you are not alone. Sometimes, the comments are a little subtler which can make it even harder to stick up for yourself because then you are called emotional or even better, crazy. Don't back down in fear of being seen as that nagging woman. Embrace it. You will be called a bitch. Embrace it. Be a bad ass bitch. You know who you are and no one can take that from you. Change your perspective and your perspective changes; being called names because others are intimidated by your intelligence can be seen as a compliment. It could feel uncomfortable but women throughout history have had to be uncomfortable in order to evoke change.

If You Want Something Big, Get Something Big. Don't Settle.

I didn't shift my career because it was male dominated. I shifted because I wasn't fulfilled emotionally nor could I see a vast and bright future for myself in photography. Having said that, perhaps if I saw more women in higher positions, I would have felt differently about it in the end. After graduating photography school in Montreal, I moved back to Toronto where I started assisting to gain experience in the field and better understand the industry. There seemed to be a few other female assistants so I didn't really see too much of a divide. But as I got farther into my years of assisting, it became apparent why women didn't stay very long in the assistant's role. I worked for one photographer who used to stroke his goatee as he peered at me which always made me a little uncomfortable since I frequently caught him staring at my chest. Then there was the day that he asked me to tape down a backdrop and then stood over me, uncomfortably close, as I was on my knees taping it down. I think back to these times and I did what most women do, grin and bear it. I was young and starting out and said photographer used to tell me how lucky I was to be working with him and that no one else would hire me. I stopped working with him and found other people to work with. I started working on large advertising shoots which I thought was great, until again, my role became very clear to me. Other male assistants didn't like working with female assistants because they thought they were physically weak (I'm sure they believed we were inferior mentally as well as physically though). I worked my ass off, pushed myself physically to be as strong and sometimes stronger than my male counterparts. I soon had a reputation for working like a guy. For a brief moment, I took pride in that, but it was short lived as it became exhausting to always have to prove myself. Many people would ask me if I was planning on becoming a producer (most women in the industry find themselves as producers or reps.). So I tried it, it wasn't for me. After I left production and went to digital operation, I had people asking me why I didn't consider becoming a rep. I started answering that question by asking "Why, because I'm a woman?!" I found some female photographers to work with and felt good going to work. What I noticed was that I was seeing more all-female sets! Great right? Well, although it was great to see and be a part of, why weren't there any women shooting the high profile jobs? I had worked with many capable female photographers but when it came to high profile ad jobs, a female photographer was like a unicorn. I'm sure there are a few women shooting large production jobs in Toronto, but the fact of the matter is that there aren't nearly enough.

Get Mad And Rise Above.

I'm sure we've all had the experience of working with a man that either hated us for merely being a woman, or wanted to fuck us because we worked in the same vicinity as them. Sometimes, both at the same time. Boys will be boys right, Wrong. Being viewed only as a sexual object is something we should not get used to. It is demeaning and lowers our self-worth and self-esteem. Battling these advances can sometimes be exhausting and seem like an upwards battle. But we have to push on in order to change the climate. And I don't mean that you have to wear turtlenecks and not be your sexy selves. Be yourself and love yourself and use it as fuel to burn even brighter. Many women have experienced men that have abused their power or authority in the workplace in order to make sexual advances upon them. Although we'd all like to believe that we would slap them in the face and walk away, that's not how it usually plays out. It is not your fault. We are so often blamed for the wrong doing of men. "She shouldn't have drank that much", "Did you see what she was wearing?" and my favorite, "She was asking for it and probably liked it". This is bullshit and we need to make sure our sons, fathers and brothers know that any of these excuses are NOT acceptable. Educating male friends and families can be the first step. Starting a dialogue can be very powerful.

You Are Too Valuable To Sell Yourself Short.

I started thinking about why I got into the photography industry and what I loved about it. I decided to get off set and get back into the creative groove. I got into retouching, or photoshopping, as most people know it. It seemed like the best fit for me. I would work from home and get to be both creative and technical. I really loved it for a while. I still enjoy it but I can't have it as my sole job. We had a baby in 2015 which turned my world upside down. I assumed that I had set myself up perfectly for having a baby. I would retouch while I was home with him and make a living. Laughable. I got a large and complicated contract when he was 4 months old. The deadlines were impossible and they offered me half of what I had quoted them but I took it anyway. Mid way through the project, I had a breakdown and had to reassess what I was doing. I was angry at my 4 month old for needing me too much, I was angry at myself for taking a pay cut and I was angry at the client for being unreasonable. My husband, who is very supportive, encouraged me to do what I felt was right and he helped me weigh my options. I had never quit a job before. It felt really good. I had to realize what I was and wasn't capable of and honor it. It was around that time that my friend, Christina, introduced me to Arbonne, a home-based network marketing business. I saw the potential in the business model, the products were (and still are) healthy for me and my family and there is a community of positive like-minded women around me. The support and encouragement of this group is invaluable.

Throughout this chapter, I've given you advice on how to overcome the stresses of inequality at work, but everyone will cope with these issues differently. My biggest piece of advice is, to not believe that it is ok or that's just how it is. Ask yourself what makes you happy and take a chance on yourself. We are so much stronger than we think we are. I climbed Mount Kilimanjaro in 2010 and before I left, someone told me something that has stuck with me still to this day. When our mind tells us to give up and that we can't go any farther, we actually have 60% left in the tank.

> We are so much stronger than we tell ourselves we are. Hold your head high and be proud to be a strong woman.

[1] It's a Man's Man's Man's World (n.d). It's a Man's Man's Man's World. Retrieved from Wikipedia Online https://en.m.wikipedia.org/wiki/It%27s_a_Man%27s_Man%27s_Man%27s_World

[2] Gilroy, R. (2016, April 12). Do women earn 79 cents of every man's dollar? Hell no, so let's stop saying it [Web Log Post] Retrieved from www.bustle.com/articles/154168-do-women-earn-79-cents-of-every-mans-dollar-Hell-no-so-let's-stop-saying-it

[3] Facts About The Gender Wage Gap In Canada. (n.d) Facts About The Gender Wage Gap In Canada. Retrieved from Canadianwomen.org Online http://www.canadianwomen.org/facts-about-the-gender-wage-gap-in-canada

[4] Carson, E. (2016). When Tech Firms Judge On Skills Alone, Women Land More Job Interviews. Retrieved from CBS News Online http://www.cbsnews.com/news/when-tech-firms-judge-on-skills-alone-women-land-more-job-interviews/

[5] McCullough, JJ. (2015, January 22). Female World Leaders Currently in Power [Web Log Post JJMcCullough.com Retrieved from http://www.jjmccullough.com/charts_rest_female-leaders.php

Chapter 16

Overcoming The Past And Embracing The Present

by Rusiana T. Mannarino

"We are products of our past, but we don't have to be prisoners of it."
~ Rick Warren

Rusiana T Mannarino

Rusiana was born in a small city in Indonesia. She spent her early twenties till mid-thirties travelling the world for work. Her exposures to different cultures and places are priceless experiences that solidified her outlook on human values and globalization. It also contributed immensely towards her many valuable skills that later helped her in her business.

Her hard work and genuine passion to help others has landed her a spot as the Top International Sponsoring Award Achiever for Canadian market in 2015 with Arbonne International. Rusiana holds a degree in Economy Management Study and completed a year post-graduate program in Global Marketing.

She is a travel addict and she loves shopping! She believes that when women stick together, they can change the world. She also believes that the best time to start making dreams come true is when we were 7 and the second best time is now! For most days, Rusiana's office is her dining table but it doesn't stop her from running her global business successfully. She is exactly where she wants to be; home with her husband and her two young children, Francesco (9) and Carina (6). They live in Montreal, Canada.

"Put your heart, mind, and soul into even our smallest acts. This is the secret of success".

-Swami Sivanada

rusiana@me.com | www.rusianatjiu.arbonne.com
fb: www.facebook.com/RusianaTMannarinoArbonne

WHEN I WAS offered to co-author this book, I was completely flabbergasted on the inside. As usual, in the split second following compliments of any kind, some of my childhood memories rushed through my mind, piled up with great accumulation of negativities.

While I was pondering the idea, I asked my husband to describe me in five sentences. This is what he said: "You are a happy soul. People are happy around you. You radiate a childlike genuine happiness. You attract people who are seeking comfort and joy. That is why I can't live without you!" (The last one didn't count though). In my mind, I was saying *"Wow, compliments! But you are wrong, I'm not whoever you just said!"* You see, destructive self-talk! How can I contribute to this book?

People in my life see me as a positive person. What they don't know is for the longest time, I didn't see myself that way. My childhood was the total opposite of *childlike genuine happiness.* How can I show people how to beat stress if I'm still recalling all these memories? For many years I was ignoring these thoughts, hoping it would go away over time. It didn't. The stress didn't either.

So, what changed? I changed. I broke up with STRESS! In this chapter, I am sharing my breakup story. My wish for you is that you will be inspired to break up with yours too. As Rick Frishman said, "Your book doesn't have to be perfect, it just has to be." So, I said YES!

Overcoming The Past: How To Accept And Let Go

"Letting go isn't about having the courage to release the past; it's about having the wisdom to embrace the present." ~ Dr. Steve Maraboli

Every adult has a childhood. We may not remember it all, but we all have some sad and happy stories to tell. Many studies have proven that childhood shapes a person's adult life. Even as an adult, we still keep a portion of us as a child at heart. Sadly, many of us may still be struggling with it. Left unattended, this can create stress and self-inflicted limitations that will prevent us from living a stress-free, peaceful life.

The next few paragraphs are moments from my childhood. The story might be disturbing for some, but remember, it was the past.

It was a sunny day. I fought with my cousin and she cried. She went to her mother and as usual it was my fault that she cried. My aunt came out upset and set up to punish me with a sapu lidi (broom made of coconut mid-ribs). I went to hide in a nearby cemetery, one of my favorite spots to hide. I was scared; I could almost hear my own heartbeat. I held back my tears; out of fear and anger I couldn't cry. A few moments passed, I didn't hear my aunt anymore but I was still too scared to come out. Then my eyes spotted some leaves in my surrounding. My grandmother used these leaves to make her black cakes. I quickly forgot about the present danger. I was thinking how happy my grandmother would be if I brought her some of these leaves. I picked up a bunch while thinking if these plants could survive without a mother, so could I. To be really safe, I then proceeded to hide under a wooden bridge. Down there, surrounded by garbage, wild plants, possibly animal and human wastes, bugs, and possibly rats, I felt really safe! I was too scared of getting caught that I didn't care about rats. That night, I still received some sapu lidi's strikes. I was 6.

My parents divorced when I was 5. By court order, I had to live with my dad, while my younger sister lived with my mother. That year, I experienced many events that I would not wish upon anyone, let alone a child. I lived with my dad and some other family members in a same house. At that very young age, I had chores varied from carrying heavy buckets of water to cleaning and moping. Strangely, I was actually happy with those chores. I felt important and useful. I didn't have many possessions but I remember my brown dress, my blue dress, my brown sandals and a few toys. No school, no routine, no mother.

My worst memory is when someone in the family molested me

on a few occasions. One time, he even brought over his friends. I was told not to tell anyone. I was confused, I was scared and I told no one. I thank God I wasn't raped. I remember swimming in the river and I almost drowned; it was then that I learned how to swim. I was asthmatic; it was then that I learned how to calm myself down by breathing slowly. I had lice and suffered from eyes allergy. I was told that my mother didn't want me, no one loved me, I was useless, ugly, and stupid and all other mean words; As a child, I believed those words.

After almost a year, my mother came to take me back when she finally heard about how I was being treated. The first time I saw her again, I didn't say a word. I was just standing, looking at her as if she was a stranger. She had long hair (without lice) and she smelled good so I decided to like her again. Went I lived with my mother and my sister and a few family members. I thought if I had a mother, no one could be mean to me anymore! I was wrong.

One day, I just came back from school. I was a proud 1st grader. Once home, my aunt who I thought was a bit scary, asked me to do some chores. I had to fill up the tub with water from the well and wash dishes. I quickly did the first but then I broke some plates while washing dishes. I was so scared my hands were shaking. I was trying to explain but I was perceived as talking back. I was punished, my hair pulled, slapped, pinched and sapu lidi strikes. That night, while I was asleep, my mother noticed all the marks and then the big fight happened. I believed I was the cause of all the fighting. I wanted to go back to the cemetery and hide under the bridge again. I was 7.

It took me awhile to be able to share these stories. As a child, stress was put on me involuntarily. I grew up mostly camouflaging my own emotions. I had low self-esteem and self-doubt. I was scared, lonely, angry and stressed. It took me a long time to get enough courage and wisdom to accept my past and to make sense out of it. Once I did, along with my religious belief, values, education, my experiences and my friends and family, I broke up with stress!

Our stories might be different, but if you feel that you are stressed by something that happened in your past, believe that you have the power to walk away from it. Some people seek professional help and some don't. Regardless, it starts with us knowing how to **accept and then to let go.**

Acceptance

As a 6-year-old in that cemetery, I knew I was wrong. I needed to hide so I wouldn't be punished! When I accepted my situation, my mind was free to find solutions and to make changes. It was then that I noticed those leaves, and I was able to feel happy in that stressful moment. Accept whatever situation we are in. We can't undo! We can do! And we will do!

Erin Olivo Ph.D. from Wise Mind Living wrote, "It may surprise you that one of the best ways to reduce stress and diffuse a stressful situation is to simply to accept it. Accept the environment you're in. Accept whatever is happening. Accept your feelings about it all. Accept that you are really stressing! Practicing this kind of acceptance works more immediately to dial down your stress level. Finding acceptance is often what allows you to be ready and able to make a necessary change."

So, how to accept gracefully as an adult?

Take an honest look of what we did without any judgment. When we made bad choices, we can't undo them, so don't add any pity, instead turn towards it and explore the possibilities to make the necessary changes. Practice accepting the past, the stress will be reduced significantly and you will be able to see other alternatives and make necessary changes.

Letting Go

It's time to make us available again! Break up with stress! Imagine that you're hanging on a monkey bar and the pain in your shoulders if you keep hanging on. It takes a lot of energy and creates physical pain. Acceptance won't be enough if we don't let go.

Hanging on does not make us safe.
Letting go does.

However, make sure the ground is safe.

How to let go? Focus on positive alternatives. By letting go, we make ourselves available again for new shiny things. As a business owner, our business is the new, shiny thing. We choose to be a business owner because we love our self while we are at it. When we love what we do, work is no longer work. Thus we have less stress and we are better at letting go.

Today, I can say I have accepted my past and I let go the negative thoughts. I forgive and I'm at peace. Even though stress is thrown at me on a daily basis, I accept and let go quickly. Stress that I have today is easier compared to what happened back then.

The funny thing is, I don't remember I was ever stressed as a child, but they were stressing me out as an adult.

I have learned to **accept and to let go**. I broke up with stress and I am ready for a change.

Embracing The Present

Embracing the present is to *be* present. It is when we use all our senses to enjoy the moment, all at the same time. When we do that, not only we are able to make good decisions, we are also free from stress!

Moving to Canada was one of my major life changing decisions. I wasn't aware how challenging it could be. Throw motherhood into it and tadaaa!!! Hello stress! I have two wonderful children and a husband whom I love very much but having them also means that I have less time for myself.

A couple of years ago, I was at the bottom of the barrel. I was on self-pity, I felt old and ugly, unhappy and stressed! Right back where I started when I was 6. I needed help. I wanted a career that suits my situation but it was non-existent.

> I came to the decision that the only way for me to build a career was to create one.

I accepted motherhood. **I let go** of the idea to find an ideal job and I took the opportunity to start my own business. **I embraced the present.**

Why Start My Own Business?

Finding a job itself is stressful enough. As a foreign, I faced more challenges:

- **Stereotyping**.
  There is a stereotype for Asian woman married to a non-Asian man. It usually means that the woman has no monetary possession or talent and the relationship is usually based on physical attraction. I personally couldn't care less on this

one, but I can't help not feel challenged. Proving something is stressful. Entering the work force with that label on my forehead is belittling, but by being my own boss, I ripped off that label.

- **Language barrier.**
  When I first arrived in Montreal, I was pretty sure that I would be fluent in French pronto. Guess what? I'm still kicking my butt on this one. The fact that I can't express myself clearly is very frustrating and stressful. Most jobs here require a bilingual person, for those who are not, they usually settle for a less paying job. By owning our own business, we have the freedom to choose who we want to work with and what language we use. It doesn't mean we don't have to learn the language. We just want the process to be not stressful.

- **Foreign qualification system on education and work experiences.**
  In most developed countries, there is a system to validate any education and work experiences. I have met a few highly educated women with degrees from other countries that were not given the same recognition. I'm not saying the system is not fair. It's a system. It's just frustrating and stressful to settle with a less paying job. Some aren't proud of what they're doing. Owning a business, no matter how small or big will give us the recognition needed.

- **Motherhood.**
  There are more and more jobs that we can do from home nowadays. Still, nothing gives me the same freedom to work around my children's schedule. Being my own boss can be challenging but it is worth the juggling.

Lastly

Getting stress out of the way prepares us to embrace the present. I am no longer waiting for magic to happen, instead, I started making my own. The present holds the most power to my future. There is no place for stress.

Now looking back, I am grateful for what happened in the past. It didn't break me; instead, I came out a survivor. I hate no one, I blame no one, and I am at peace. I thank God for the path he has given me, so I can appreciate what I have today and know when to say enough.

Stress is a state of mind; it is not the real problem. Problem simply means a lack of solution. Find the solution and there will be no problem. When there is no problem, there will be no stress.

I accept the past. I let go. I embrace the present.

Section 5

———◆✖◆———

The Breakup with No Re-Return!

by

Ky-Lee Hanson

IT'S STRESSFUL TO deal with stress but if we are passive towards stress, it leads to depression and anxiety. One may feel lonely, isolated, demotivation and lose the joy in life. They may become worried about dealing with the stressful situation and create a perception that is far from reality. They may feel getting things off their chest will cause more stress based on the reaction from the other person.

Time alone is important for the soul but it is very different than feeling isolated. One should feel connected to them-self and comfortable in their daily interactions with others. Speak your mind with ease to get to the outcome you desire. I often wonder if one lived detached from society would they still face stress. I am sure they would. However, would it be the same and to what level? How much stress comes through our interactions with another person? How much is social? How much stems from a misunderstanding or different views? Can we live in society and have a happy stress free life? Free of bad stress that is, some stress is good. We can feel excited, anxious and nervous but in a good way. We may worry or second guess deadlines or projects, things may not always go smoothly but learning isn't easy. It is rewarding but can also come with its own stress.

Communication is the answer to many situations. Talking out issues and growing from them. Sometimes when confronted, you need to take some time to yourself, read, think, listen to your emotions, and your body's actions. Do you feel sad, in a slump, with heavy eyes and closed off? Your emotional defense system in response to a stressful situation may have built a wall around you. You aren't ready to deal with the confrontation but until you do, you may feel stuck. Your energy may be low and you feel depressed.

We have heard from our authors on how to identify, manage and end overwhelming-stress in various situations including inner battles, the household, the workplace, between family and friends and stress we experience from disease and finances. Ideally, now you want to control the bad and embrace the good. You may have identified some of your

Stress symptoms. Feeling tired, bloated, skin issues, overheating, can be signs of something else or can be from mental stress and your body reacting to it. Maybe you are tired of going to the doctor again and again, and it could be time to manage stress to elevate some of your symptoms.

My Naturopath told me we spend so much of our time disconnected from our body. We are in our minds, floating along. It's common when people sit at a computer, watch TV etc., although possibly mentally stimulating and you feel good, we tend to sit incorrectly, our breathing slows down and we aren't getting enough oxygen. We may get lost in a technology trance and skip meals, not drink enough water, which could lead to deficiencies and other problems.

If you do not feel your best or are unsure you even know what "best" feels like, breaking up with stress might be a good place to start. You feel empowered and capable to do so. You are ready! From here, what is going to keep you from moving forward instead of rolling back into a stress slump?

In our closing chapter, I will walk you through some of my story as the coauthors have previously done. My story and steps aim to help you find your WHY, your motivation and gain momentum towards controlling your life. The focus here is to gain a clear and empowered mind. To be open to change and embrace everything that comes along with that. I believe in growing-PAINS. The law of the Universe is, there is a negative to every positive and vice versa. To get to the good, we sometimes first need to go through the bad. If we are prepared and accept that this is life, I believe that sets us up for an optimistic mind, helps us to create contingency plans and awareness. If we can take challenges as learning experiences instead of defeats, we are more educated. Knowledge is power and power is control.

Chapter 17

If It Does Not Evolve Me, Then It Does Not Involve Me.

By Ky-Lee Hanson

"Stress comes from who you think you should be.

Peace comes from being who you are. "

~ Unknown

Ky-Lee Hanson
Bosswoman | Visionary | Creator
of Opportunity & Motivation

Ky-Lee Hanson is the kind of girl who was glad to turn 30. She is an old soul who gets the big picture. She is built on hope and believes in equality. She is optimistic but understands things for what they really are. Ky-Lee enjoys people. She finds people fascinating. Being someone who can spot potential, one of the hardest things she ever had to learn was, "You can't help someone who doesn't want to help themselves."

Growing up, she had a hard time understanding why people couldn't seem to live the lives they dreamed of. Often thinking she must be the main character on a show like The Truman Show because nothing seemed to make sense. She always saw things differently and found it hard to relate to people which ended up sending her into a downward spiral in her twenties when she felt she had no choice but to settle. She felt suppressed, limited and angry. Ky-Lee has the ability to hyper focus and learn things quickly. She has a power-mind and found the true strength of life through a serious health battle in her late twenties. Ky-Lee took control and for years, mastered how to get her power back.

Ky-Lee is a business and motivational mentor. Her studies in sociology, human behavior, stress management, nutrition and health sciences has led her to have a deep understanding of people. She thrives on creating opportunities to help people along their journey of becoming the best versions of themselves. Ky-Lee has an open door policy she learnt from her Mom, a listening ear and an opportunity to link arms and take you down your Golden Brick Road.

Coauthor with her: www.gbragency.com
ig: @kylee.hanson.bosswoman | fb: facebook.com/kylee.hanson

MOTIVATION DOES NOT always come from a place of desire; it can also come from a place of fear. I believe motivation to be the fuel for our momentum. When living in momentum, it is a state of moving towards desire, a state that is happy and exciting. It is easy to desire but how do we *actually* create momentum towards obtaining our desires and our dream life? Deep down, we need something that ignites that momentum. A train is often a metaphor for momentum. It takes a lot of coal and steam, and effort to get going. What within you is deeper than desire? What do you fear? What is your big dark pit of burning coal? What to you, totally sucks? Here, I believe is where we find our motivation. Personally, what keeps me going is knowing exactly what I *do not* want for my life. I am so focused on not letting my life go to that bad place, I've been there, and I hate it! I am a lover, not a hater; So for me, I cannot survive in that bad place.

My bad place is stale, it is confusing, it is lonely, it is sick and it has addictions as distractions. This place is under stress, full of worry and anxiety. It is not a place for thriving or for self-confidence, it is a place of judgement and full of toxic people and their misery trying to keep me as its company. It is a place of control and I am not the one in-charge.

People ask me how I am so motivated. Anyone that knows me will tell you how dedicated I am. It took me 31 years to figure out why I am so motivated. My life has never been a walk in the park. To some, it may look like that now, but I have had my share of struggles. I work so hard to not struggle and it has come down to managing two things: self-confidence and expectations.

Growing up, my life was a bit all over the place. I have always been a motivated and dedicated person. Self-esteem was rarely an issue for me. I knew I was meant for something, I have worth and was always open to seize every opportunity but I just didn't know where I fit in. Where I fell short was the self-confidence; the experience, knowledge and assurance of what I could handle and what I was actually good at.

As a preteen, my dad left, and there was complete disconnection in my extended family. I had to grow up quickly. My younger sisters and nephews were a responsibility, money was tight and a lot of dreams couldn't happen for me or for us, as a family. I grew up in small towns (before social media), so I was lacking a certain exposure to mentors and inspiring people. I have always been a risk taker and a dreamer, but never really had the experience of having a coach, a team or anyone, invest their time and effort into me. In high school, I didn't make the basketball team, dance groups or anything related to singing. I didn't land many of the chances I took. I quickly became a write off "you will never amount to anything", because I couldn't get things complete. I just wasn't interested in what they were **telling me** to do. I had zero career and college options. I am self-diagnosed with ADHD, which most successful people have, but for me it was never harnessed properly until I was in my 30's. I realize now that my brain seems to just go a million miles faster than most people and was the cause of a lot of the emotional disconnection I've experienced and my inability to accept things at face value.

In my young adulthood, I fell into that bad place. It's not because of something someone did, or didn't do. It completely has everything to do with expectations. The expectations I set for myself, that I set for others which they never [chose to or couldn't] live up to and the mediocre expectations people set of me. I had expectations for my father to be a part of my whole life but he isn't and I transferred that let down and fear of abandonment onto most of my relationships and friendships in life. In school, when I was told I couldn't do something, I became sad, angry and felt defeated. *People say I can't but how come others can, why don't I get a dream life?* I began to build resistance towards "shooting for the stars". I stopped speaking my dreams, that way, I could avoid ridicule. I stopped trying. If I tucked my dreams inside, no one could lower my expectations, I could keep them.

Starting out as an adult, I was really good at partying... big achievement... but it did help me find two of the most important things in my life. I met my spouse and I started my first business in event marketing. I was good at it. I LOVED to bring people together which has always been my strongest skill. I remember how strange I thought it was when people wanted to be my friend or when people said I was good at something. It was as if they were speaking a different language. I knew I could do a lot but I felt that kind of life wasn't for me. I wasn't born into success, fame or education. How could I dare want to be a scientist and an author one day - I am just a party girl. I am not smart.

It took me 8 more years of living in this bad place, this dark place in my mind. I thought the world was dark around me, and at times, in certain environments, it was but looking back, it was my pain clouding my judgement. It was the control that these unrealistic expectations had over me. I knew I was capable but I had learnt to assume that I just wasn't meant for anything special. People had it better than me. I remember being so angry at times and so stressed out. I was under so much pressure to conform and just live a mediocre life with a mediocre job. There was no spark. Inside, I was a total stress case and on the outside, my words were negative.

There is a key point that separates a peaceful life from a stressful life. I now know that key to be the difference between having hope or having expectations for your life. An expectation is defined as a belief that is centered on the future, which may or may not be realistic. A less advantageous result gives rise to the emotion of disappointment. We all want the best for ourselves and often feel life isn't fair. The truth is, it's not fair but it is possible of change.

We may expect a lot for our future and spend much time being disappointed that we are not there yet. Some choose to give up and settle while others remain angry and looking for someone or something to blame. We may go our whole lives in a state of wrongful acceptance or pointing the finger, but I am here to show you life can completely change and you *do* have the control to do that.

How Can We Bridge From A Place Of Darkness To A Place Of Light?

For me, it was illness. It took a huge life rattling personal experience for me to realize I had no choice but to take control. It was that or cancer. I was so lost for years while sick, scared shitless. *This was really all my life had set out for me.* It took a second scare for me to shift into a "no matter what" state. You know what I did? What I FINALLY did? The bridge from a place of darkness to a place of light is *asking for help.* I asked every single question possible that came to my mind about my health. I asked the internet, I asked 500 million doctors and alternative doctors, bloggers, friends and social media. It consumed me. Guess what, by asking, I got educated, I grew and I got better. I was like a sponge! I remember finally having some moments of clarity in my life and it was because I was becoming educated on "the self". I could start to look at my life differently and identify what was stressing me out; limitations, money, eating the wrong foods, doing the wrong job, high estrogen = STRESS! I wanted to be healthy and healthy to me meant happy.

Give Yourself Just One Thing – An Inquisitive Mind

Become obsessed with what you want to change and put your focus there. You can keep it to yourself by reading books, *good job*, and you can ask for confidential, non judgement help from people like me and I recommend nutrition, therapy and most important is a positive circle of influence.

If this chapter doesn't speak to you, if you are not in a dark place, someone close to you is. Don't be afraid to ask them what they really need. People just need to be listened to in a constructive manner, this is how the healing process begins.

Controlling Your External And Internal Environment

I don't live in this bad place anymore, but in a second I can go back and I know the difference. This is where my motivation comes from; knowing that I will not go back there and only I can control that. My motivation is to never be that angry stressed-out person again and my momentum is my own happiness. Let's hope it doesn't take a huge life rattling illness to shake you out of your slump. Maybe you have been living in this bad place for decades. This bad place invites me in from time to time within my relationships and within my growing career. Around certain people, it's as if I'm on an extended stay in this place.

In my coaching business, I coach on the **Influence of 5**. It is based on a concept taught by many including Jim Rohn. The immediate people around us, *plus the occasional troll on social media,* cause us the most stress. Some stress is good, it can be motivating and it can mean we are growing. Right now though, I am talking about the kind of stress that makes you anxious, that makes you tired, sad or angry. Influence of 5 is the five closest people to you on a daily basis. Look at your text messages, emails, recent phone list and social media chats. Include a coworker that you may work closely with. Who are the most frequent five? Are these people in your corner or are you in theirs? Your most frequent five have more influence on you than anything else in the world. We need to make sure these five know our truth and see the best version of us. They often see more in us than we do. They are either in it with us or they are leading us. Our Influence of 5 needs to be an inspiring bunch. I am not suggesting that you stop helping people or remove other people. Your energy may just need to be reallocated so you can fit in an inspiring Influence of 5.

You Need To Call "Objection!" On Judgey People

During my self-discovery, I faced a lot of obstacles from the people around me. Time and time again, family and friends said, "You are able to do what you do because of your spouse". These jerks are trying to steal my power! You know what you do, you silent treatment their ass. Go back to your constructive methods: reading, your projects, your Influence of 5 and get pumped back up. In all fairness, what they said had some merit. My spouse makes a great income but guess what, during his career development, I was the one who worked and supported us. I was the one that encouraged and designed his business. Without me and without him, together as a partnership, his greatness would not be the same. I know in my heart that my journey is MY journey. I would have ended up here no matter what. I CHOSE to self-discover and grow. Every person has the same opportunity I did. We can read books, we can ask for wisdom, we can make mistakes and choose to learn from them. People on the outside do not see the full story, they just see what is now and judge you based on that. People see what they want to see and most people only live on the outcome and take for granted the stepping stones. They will always judge you and really what they are doing is comparing themselves and rationalizing as to why you have something they don't. You have to not listen to them and own your power.

The pressures and expectations that your family, friends, coworkers and society have on you are greatly influenced by the expectations you have of yourself. When I started embracing my small successes, I felt more confident! I felt happier, I felt successful! As I focused on small successes and shared those with people, their tune began to change also. There will be some people that will still try to knock you down; instead of falling over and picking yourself back up, just stop falling over! You know you achieved and you know within you that you are growing. Other people really do not matter.

I have learnt to protect myself. To display my strength. It was extremely hard and you need to essentially *break up* with your expectations of others. You can not make them be nice and you can not make them listen, so stop trying. I focus on positive influence from motivated people. If you move to Australia, you will start speaking like an Aussie right? Same with what surrounds you today. If everyone has a "can't do attitude", you will likely pick up on that. If you are always building a safety net around you from these people, you will always be trapped there.

Dig Deep And Get Messy

We all know any kind of break up is messy. A break up happens because you have **identified what you do not want**, remember, this is how you find motivation and now you need to put it into action. You go into a state of momentum - it's happening - and now you are focused on the desire of a positive outcome. Breaking up with stress is no different. You probably need to have a breaking point and it might look like a nervous breakdown. Identifying fear and desire is not a relaxed process, you need to transition and detox your emotions. You must persevere!

Would it be easier to not deal with the growing pains, the stress, the self-expectations and let downs that perseverance brings? Is this maybe a reason why people are afraid of change? Think hard about what you do not want in your life as well as what you truly want, even if it seems farfetched. What is the process in-between to keep distance from the fear and get closer to the desire? The real trick to a happy life is to enjoy the journey while moving towards achieving desire.

If we can end pressure and manage our self-expectations; from there, we can control our external environment and projected pressures and expectations from, and of, others. Imagine where a structured, positive and flourishing way of life could take us. We then could grow into the dream life we are meant to have.

In my business, I am essentially a giver of opportunity. I am a Motivational Mentor and Business Creationist. One would be amazed at the amount I get turned down. I really learn a lot about people with what I do. Often I hear, "I am just not motivated like you are", "What if it doesn't work", "You work all the time" and "I can't do what you do". Hmm, in other words "Ky-Lee, it's not you, it's me". People do not realize they are standing in their own way. They are standing in the way of their greatness. I feel many people do not understand what freedom looks like and that it is possible.

I was a trapped young person, full of potential that no one saw and often in my adulthood, I have felt "looked over" also. It's always been up to ME and it took time to learn this. I am not an opportunist; I am more of an altruist. My mission in life is to help other people like myself - which I believe in some way to be everyone - live their dream life.

I am a prime example of change and perseverance, I see myself as an expert at motivation and taking risks. I am extremely successful at business but I wasn't always in the traditional sense of making money. Sir Richard Brandon, creator of the Virgin empire, philanthropist and public figure, says his first publications business was his most successful. Financially no, quite the opposite but he says it taught him everything he knew and put the right people in place for him to grow his empire. He says it was the most successful because he learnt about people which lead to everything he has now. It is 100% about how you perceive your work. Make your work matter.

You Have To Go Through The Obstacles To Be Strong Enough To Best Utilize The Success.

Imagine waking up one day and all your dreams are fulfilled. Wow! Amazing but how do you manage it all? Right now, you WANT the "wake up one day to success scenario". You have self-expectations that you deserve this. Many people skip over the details. If we do not know the inner workings of this dream life, we won't know how to live it.

We must cultivate the environment of the dream for it to become reality.

You may have heard, "it's all in the detail". A big shift for me was learning to have long term telescope vision, but also, short term microscope vision. What are the steps to take to get to the dream? What are milestones that build towards the dream? These milestones prepare you for greatness.

Make Your Daily Habits Into Daily Achievements

Most people analyze their life over a 1 year period. When I started a sales business, life became about monthly performance. Every end of month is like New Year's Eve. I reflect on the previous month, crush goals in those final hours and the next day, the 1st of the month, I set my monthly resolutions and break them down into weeks and days. I began to see a ton of success, personal growth and a financial explosion. Try to be less passive with time.

Approach tasks as achievements, and at the end of the day, discussing with partners will really sets a "cheerleader" mentality. You feel successful, you learn each day and get better and better. It becomes a routine, a habit and then a way of life.

Momentum comes from positive daily habits, or, daily achievements. Momentum is something you create. There is no other way to get it. If you can learn to recognize the rush of having momentum, you can clearly identify when you do not have it. Momentum is moving towards the desire.

Fall in love with the journey and be grateful for the growth from each small step. As we go along on our "way to success", we learn a lot! Unfortunately, a lot is taken for granted because it's not "THE" dream... If you are always focused on what you don't have, you will never have enough.

The Way To Move Forward Is To Stop Having Expectations

Happiness is freedom and freedom is happiness. What is freedom to you? To me, it is control. The ability to be the one that makes my decisions, not a boss, a loved one or a social restriction. ME. Create freedom within yourself and freedom from other people. If you can keep yourself in a place of daily achievement and gratitude, focus on self-growth each and every day, you will begin to control the direction of your life.

Create focus, create a plan. Start building your dream life. You do need to construct it; it will NEVER simply show up. Don't get caught up on "what should be", "what has been" or comparing yourself to others. Don't set yourself up for disappointment because you are expecting things to turn out a certain way. Become excited for the best possible scenario but also be prepared for impact.

When we stop being caught up in expectations, we can begin to enjoy the now, embrace the growth and construct our dream life on a solid foundation.

Acknowledgements

I would like to thank all the people in my life who have believed in me to be their leader, mentor, coach or support system, and as such have come to me for advice or guidance. It has encouraged me to be the best version of myself and has forced me to make many hard yet rewarding decisions in my life. Because of you, I push on even at times when it would seem easier not to. I would also like to acknowledge the people that have challenged me. We learn the most through other people's actions and words. We can take it on as personal stress or we can analyze what is really happening in the situation and find that other people's perception is not our reality. These individuals have helped me to find assurance within - that pain needs to exist for us to celebrate and embrace joy. Every person who has given me feedback through constructive criticism has helped shape what I am today, and this book is one act of deliverance.

Thank you to Matty for believing in my ability to do this months - and I am sure even years - before I saw it for myself. Thank you to all the amazing risk-taking contributing authors in this book. They believed in a vision. It did not take seeing to believe. This is what makes them the best Women for the job!

~ Ky-Lee Hanson

Thanks to my husband Rohit, for his unwavering confidence and support in everything that I do. - Supriya Gade

Thank you to my husband Alan, for believing in the lioness within me, and my mom for nurturing my dreams. - Tania J. Moraes-Vaz

A HUGE thanks to the love of my life, my hubby, for encouraging me to reach for the stars. -Sunit Suchdev

Thanks to my fiancé Scott for your unwavering support, your belief in my abilities and always responding "It's up to you" when I ask, "Should I do it?" - Lauren Karatanevski

Thanks to my husband Mark who supports me in everything I try and my daughters who came on this adventure with me. - Patricia Yeatman

Thank you to all my amazing clients, my team, my family for inspiring me to always follow my dreams. I hold you dear to my heart. - Eva Macias

Thank you to my daughter for always inspiring me and my family for their endless support. - Kelly Rolfe

Thanks to my support system Maurice, Christine, Elnaz and Monica for standing by me, and believing in me. - AJ Roy

Thank you to my mother, Debra. Your strength, compassion and tenacity have made me into the person I am today. - Michelle Zubrinich

Many thanks given to my husband Trevor for his support along the way - Karina Ullrich

Acknowledgements

Thanks to all the rockstars in my organization for giving me the kick I needed to take upon this project. - Rusiana T Mannarino

I want to thank all the strong women in my life who encourage me to move forward daily, out of my comfort zone. - Stephanie Butler

Thank you to my daughter Sophia Simone for guiding me back to myself. - Kathryn Yeatman

Thanks to my daughter, the warrior who built my purpose through her strength. And to my family and friends who support me unconditionally. - Kyla Thomson

I give thanks to my three beautiful children and my love, Brent, for always believing in me no matter what my dream may be. - Amanda Yeatman

Thanks to my husband Seth for always supporting my dreams, no matter how wild and crazy they may seem. - Kimberly Francis

Golden Brick Road
Publishing House

At Golden Brick Road, we work with Dreamers.

We help those that are natural born leaders, step out and shine! Even if they do not yet fully see it for themselves. We believe in empowering each individual who will then go and inspire an entire community. Our Director, Ky-Lee Hanson, calls this The Inspiration Trickle Effect.

We help you develop and diversify your personal brand in a unique way. We want to share your story so it will inspire the world to be better. We help you develop within a joint venture project that is designed to earn you residual income and residual leads. Yes, that's right - we pay our coauthors royalties from book sales. We bring attention to what makes YOU unique and how you can make that your success. Your success is ours and vice versa. We are a publications company and a marketing agency that is backed by the most supportive community and we truly become a family.

If you want to be a public figure that is focused on helping people and providing value but you do not want to embark on the journey alone, than this is the project for you.

To inquire about writing opportunities or to bring your own idea into vision, reach out to us at www.gbragency.com